How to Think Like a Cow

The fascinating story of the first cow to be nominated for the Nobel Prize

Daniel Adrien Laverdière

Preface

I never imagined I would find myself in this situation. For decades, I have been a writer, weaving tales of science fiction adventure, romance, and the intricacies of human nature. My life was filled with words, characters, and the satisfaction of seeing my stories come to life. I thought I understood the world, or at least the human world, until the day everything changed.

It started like any other morning. I sat at my desk, sipping coffee, my fingers poised over the keyboard. But as I began to type, a strange sensation washed over me. My vision blurred, my hands felt heavy, and a bizarre transformation overtook me. In an instant, I was no longer a man. I was a cow, somewhere in an unknown pasture.

Yes, you read that correctly. A cow. A large, lumbering, grass-munching bovine. My once articulate thoughts were replaced by an overwhelming urge to graze, and the world appeared vastly different from this new perspective. The familiar sights and sounds of my home became foreign, and I found myself navigating life on four legs.

At first, I was terrified and confused. How does one adjust from crafting narratives to chewing cud? But as the days turned into weeks, I began to accept my new reality. I learned to appreciate the simple pleasures of a cow's life – the fresh taste of morning dew on grass, the comfort of the herd, and the beauty of the natural world untainted by human complexities.

This unexpected journey has given me a unique insight into a world I had never truly considered. As I adapted to my new existence, I began to see parallels between my old life and the life of a cow. Patience, routine, social bonds – these are not just human experiences but universal truths that connect all living beings.

"How to Think Like a Cow" is my attempt to bridge the gap between our species. It is a reflection on what it means to live simply, to find joy in the mundane, and to understand the profound wisdom that can come from embracing a different perspective. Whether you are a fellow writer, a curious reader, or someone seeking a fresh outlook on life, I invite you to join me on this extraordinary journey.

Let us step into the hooves of a cow and explore the world anew. You may be surprised at what you discover – not just about cows, but about yourself.

Sincerely, Daniel Adrien Laverdière

Introduction

My Transformation: From Author to Cow

As an erudite author steeped in the labyrinthine complexities of human thought and narrative, the metamorphosis I underwent is nothing short of extraordinary. The sudden, surreal shift from a sentient human being, deeply embedded in the intricate dance of words and ideas, to a bovine creature roaming the pastoral expanses, is a tale that defies the conventions of reality and demands introspection.

In the serene cocoon of my study, surrounded by tomes of literary giants and the comforting hum of a world I understood, I was preparing to embark on another literary journey. The morning was like any other—mundane yet imbued with the promise of creativity. My fingers poised over the keyboard, I was ready to weave another tapestry of words. But fate, with its inexorable and often unfathomable designs, had other plans.

An inexplicable sensation, a profound shift, ensnared my consciousness. My vision, once sharp and discerning, blurred into a kaleidoscope of unfamiliar shapes. My limbs, adept at manipulating the delicate mechanics of writing, transformed into heavy, ungainly appendages. In a flash, my identity dissolved, and I found myself embodying the essence of a cow—a creature whose existence I had scarcely considered beyond the periphery of human utility.

This bizarre and disconcerting transformation thrust me into a realm where human cognition and bovine simplicity coalesce. Initially, a cacophony of terror and confusion overwhelmed my senses. How does one transition from the complexity of human thought to the ostensibly rudimentary existence of a cow? Yet, as the days meandered on, I discovered a profound tranquility in this new state of being—a serenity born from the acceptance of the present moment and the eschewal of existential quandaries.

As a cow, my perception of time transformed. The relentless march of hours, days, and years, which had once governed my life, dissipated into the gentle ebb and flow of natural rhythms. The past, with its triumphs and tribulations, receded into oblivion. The future, a nebulous and often daunting prospect, lost its grip on my psyche. I was enveloped in the immediacy of the present—each moment a singular experience, unburdened by the weight of anticipation or regret.

This newfound existence granted me an intimate acquaintance with the sensory richness of the world. The grass beneath my hooves was not merely a green expanse but a tapestry of textures and scents, each blade a unique entity. The sky, a vast canvas above, resonated with the subtleties of light and shadow, each nuance a testament to the beauty of simplicity. My interactions with the herd revealed a complex social structure, an intricate ballet of relationships and hierarchies that mirrored, in its own way, the convolutions of human society.

Through this transformation, I began to comprehend the essence of bovine intelligence. It is not the cerebral machinations of human cognition but a profound, instinctual wisdom—a deep-seated understanding of one's place within the natural order. This wisdom, unencumbered by the trappings of ambition or desire, fosters a state of contentment and harmony.

"How to Think Like a Cow" is an exploration of this unique perspective. It is a journey into the heart of a bovine existence, where the simplicity of life is celebrated and the burdens of human complexity are cast aside. This book is not merely an account of my transformation but an invitation to embrace a different way of thinking—one that values the present, cherishes the natural world, and finds joy in the mundane.

As you turn the pages, I invite you to shed your preconceptions and immerse yourself in the world as seen through the eyes of a cow. You may discover, as I have, that there is profound wisdom to be found in the simplest of lives, and that by thinking like a cow, we can find a path to greater peace, understanding, and fulfillment.

Why Think Like a Cow?

In the cacophonous theater of human existence, where the relentless pursuit of progress and the ceaseless demands of modernity often conspire to erode our tranquility, the notion of thinking like a cow may appear, at first glance, to be a whimsical diversion or a pastoral reverie. Yet, upon deeper contemplation, one may uncover a profound, transformative philosophy within the bovine paradigm—a philosophy that offers a sanctuary from the existential turbulence of our frenetic lives.

To think like a cow is to embrace a radical simplicity, a deliberate shedding of the superfluous complexities that encumber the human spirit. Cows, in their unassuming grandeur, epitomize a mode of existence that is at once harmonious and unhurried. They are creatures whose lives are governed by the rhythms of nature rather than the artificial constructs of human society. In adopting a cow's perspective, we are invited to reconnect with the fundamental essence of being, to find solace in the present moment, and to cultivate a serene mindfulness that is often elusive in our hurried world.

The bovine experience is one of profound attunement to the immediate environment. Cows do not ruminate on the past nor fret about the future; their awareness is anchored in the present. This temporal alignment fosters a state of equanimity and contentment that is enviable. In our own lives, beset by the incessant flux of time, the ability to anchor oneself in the now can be a panacea for the anxieties and stresses that plague us. By thinking like a cow, we learn to savor each moment, to appreciate the nuances of our surroundings, and to find beauty in the mundane.

Moreover, the cow's perspective encourages a deep, intuitive connection with the natural world. In a time when humanity's estrangement from nature is contributing to ecological crises and personal disquiet, the cow offers a model for harmonious coexistence. Cows navigate their environment with a gentle respect and an intrinsic understanding of their place within the ecosystem. They engage with their surroundings in a way that is both symbiotic and sustainable. By emulating this natural attunement, we can foster a greater sense of environmental stewardship and a more profound appreciation for the interconnectedness of all life.

In the realm of social interaction, cows exhibit a communal intelligence that transcends the superficiality of human relationships. Their social structures are built on cooperation, mutual support, and an unspoken yet palpable bond of kinship. This organic solidarity contrasts starkly with the often transactional and fragmented nature of human connections. Thinking like a cow invites us to prioritize genuine, meaningful relationships, to cultivate empathy, and to engage with others in a spirit of collective harmony.

Furthermore, the cow's approach to problem-solving and learning is characterized by patience and persistence. They do not rush to conclusions nor succumb to frustration; instead, they navigate challenges with a calm, methodical perseverance. This bovine tenacity is a valuable lesson for us, encouraging a more measured and thoughtful approach to the obstacles we face in life. It teaches us that resilience is born from patience and that true understanding comes from persistent, incremental exploration.

Ultimately, to think like a cow is to embrace a philosophy of being that is rooted in simplicity, presence, and harmony. It is a conscious rejection of the frenetic pace and fragmented focus that so often define contemporary life. It is an invitation to slow down, to breathe deeply, and to immerse ourselves in the richness of the present moment.

As you embark on this journey through the pages of "How to Think Like a Cow," I urge you to open your mind and heart to the wisdom of the bovine way. Allow yourself to be transformed by the insights gleaned from this humble yet profound perspective. In doing so, you may discover a path to greater peace, contentment, and fulfillment—a path that, while simple, is imbued with the deepest wisdom of all: the wisdom of living fully and authentically in the present.

How This Book is Structured, Cowly Speaking

Ladies and gentlemen, fellow cud-chewers and hay enthusiasts, welcome to the utterly moovelous world of bovine wisdom. You may be wondering how on Earth (or in the pasture) a book could possibly be structured to capture the essence of thinking like a cow. Fear not, for I am here to guide you through this delightful journey, hoof by hoof. So, grab a tuft of grass, settle into a cozy spot under a tree, and let me explain, cowly speaking, how this book is laid out.

First up, we've got **Chapter 1: The Present Moment**. Now, cows are experts at living in the now. While humans are busy stressing about their emails and deadlines, we cows are savoring every bite of grass and every minute of sunshine. In this chapter, you'll learn how to moo-ve past your worries and bask in the simple joys of life, just like we do.

In **Chapter 2: Sensory Perception**, we delve into the incredible world of cow senses. You see, while humans rely on their gadgets and gizmos, we cows have a finely tuned sense of smell and taste that puts sommeliers to shame. This chapter will teach you to appreciate the rich tapestry of scents and flavors around you. Spoiler alert: it's not just about the grass, although that is pretty great.

Moving on to **Chapter 3: Daily Life and Routine**, where we explore the beauty of a well-ordered cow day. Grazing, chewing cud, socializing with the herd—it's all about balance, my friends. By the end of this chapter, you'll be an expert in the art of relaxation and routine, mastering the delicate dance of productivity and leisure.

In **Chapter 4: Emotional Intelligence**, we uncover the surprisingly complex emotional lives of cows. Yes, we have feelings too! From the joy of a sunny day to the sadness of a rainy one, we're in touch with our emotions. This chapter will help you moo-ve through your own emotional ups and downs with grace and aplomb.

Chapter 5: Communication and Interaction is all about how we cows convey our thoughts and feelings. Forget emojis and text messages; we use vocalizations, body language, and the occasional nudge to get our point across. You'll learn the subtle art of bovine communication and how to apply it to your own social interactions. Warning: excessive mooing may ensue.

Next, we have **Chapter 6: Connection to Nature**, where we celebrate our deep bond with the great outdoors. While humans might need apps to remind them to go outside, we cows live and breathe nature. This chapter will inspire you to reconnect with the earth, the sky, and everything in between, no hoofprints required.

In **Chapter 7: Health and Well-being**, we focus on the physical and mental wellness of cows. From our diet to our exercise routines (yes, even cows have them), you'll learn how to adopt a healthier, more balanced lifestyle. Just remember, it's all about grazing, not grazing on junk food.

Chapter 8: Reflections on Human Life takes a look at the moo-re serious side of things, drawing lessons from my days as an esteemed author. You'll find practical advice on applying bovine wisdom to your daily grind, making life simpler and more enjoyable. After all, if a cow can do it, so can you!

In **Chapter 9: The Ethical Cow**, we tackle some serious issues with a light touch. Ethical treatment of animals, compassion, empathy—it's all here. This chapter will leave you feeling more thoughtful and maybe a bit more moo-ved to make the world a better place.

Chapter 10: Cows in Culture and History is our grand tour of the rich tapestry of bovine influence throughout the ages. From mythological sacred cows to modern-day mascots, we cows have always been a big deal. This chapter will give you a greater appreciation for our moo-sive impact on human culture.

Finally, **Chapter 11: The Present and Future** wraps things up with some forward-looking thoughts. Embrace the present, let go of the past, and moo-ve confidently into the future with the wisdom of a cow. It's all about living fully and authentically, one hoof-step at a time.

So there you have it! A structured, cow-centric journey through the realms of bovine brilliance. Grab your favorite patch of grass, take a deep breath, and get ready to dive into the world of "How to Think Like a Cow." You'll laugh, you'll learn, and who knows—you might just find yourself moo-ving to a different beat.

Chapter 1: The Present Moment
Living in the Now

Ah, the present moment—a concept that philosophers have pondered, poets have romanticized, and cows have mastered. While humans are busy ticking off to-do lists and planning for a future that never quite arrives, we cows have a knack for basking in the here and now. We don't need mindfulness apps or meditation retreats; we've got the art of living in the moment down to an udder science.

You see, for a cow, life is a symphony of now. The past? It's just a moo-mory. The future? A distant moo-sical note. What matters is the luscious blade of grass right in front of us, the warm sun on our backs, and the gentle rustle of the breeze in the meadow. This is the essence of cow zen—a state of being where the present moment is all that exists, and it's gloriously sufficient.

Imagine, if you will, the simple pleasure of grazing. Each bite of grass is an event unto itself, a burst of flavor and texture that demands full attention. We savor each mouthful, chew thoughtfully, and relish the experience. There's no rush, no urgency—just the pure, unadulterated enjoyment of the present.

Living in the now isn't just about eating, though that's a significant part of our bovine existence. It's also about being fully present in our surroundings. When we wander the pasture, we don't just walk—we explore. Each step is a new adventure, each scent a story, each sound a melody. Our senses are attuned to the world around us, and we immerse ourselves in the richness of our environment.

And let's talk about rest. Humans often see rest as a luxury, something to squeeze in between bouts of productivity. But for us cows, rest is an integral part of life. We find a cozy spot, lie down, and simply be. We don't worry about the next task or fret over unfinished business. We embrace rest wholeheartedly, knowing that it's as essential to our well-being as grazing.

Now, you might be thinking, "That's all well and good for a cow, but how do I, a busy human, live in the now?" Well, my friend, it's simpler than you think. Start by noticing the small things—the taste of your morning coffee, the feel of the sun on your skin, the sound of leaves rustling in the wind. Take a cue from us cows and immerse yourself in these moments. Let go of the past and future, and give the present your full attention.

Next, slow down. Humans are always in a hurry, rushing from one thing to the next. But there's a certain magic in taking your time. Eat slowly, walk leisurely, breathe deeply. When you slow down, you begin to see the world with fresh eyes. You notice details that were once overlooked and experience life more fully.

And finally, embrace rest. Don't see it as a guilty pleasure but as a vital part of your day. Find a comfortable spot, relax, and just be. Clear your mind of worries and let yourself enjoy the simple act of resting. Trust me, your body and mind will thank you.

Living in the now is about more than just being present; it's about finding joy in the simplicity of life. It's about appreciating the little things, savoring each moment, and letting go of the constant need to do more, be more, and have more. It's about finding contentment in the here and now, just as we cows do.

So, as you journey through this chapter, take a moment to slow down, breathe, and immerse yourself in the present. Let the worries of the past and the anxieties of the future fade away. Embrace the now with open arms and an open heart. You'll find that there's a world of wonder to be discovered when you live like a cow—fully present, fully alive, and   utterly   content.

The Joy of Simple Pleasures

Welcome, dear reader, to the heart of bovine bliss—the joy of simple pleasures. While humans often chase after grand achievements and extravagant delights, we cows have a delightful secret: the most profound happiness is found in the simplest of things. In our tranquil, grass-strewn world, joy is not a destination but a journey, a series of small, delightful moments that make up the tapestry of our lives.

Consider, for a moment, the sheer delight of a fresh patch of grass. To a cow, it's not just food—it's a veritable feast of flavor, a symphony of textures, a sensory experience that demands our full attention. We don't just graze; we relish. Each bite is an exploration, each chew a meditation. The grass is green, the sun is warm, and all is right in our world.

Then there's the joy of a good scratch. Oh, the bliss of finding just the right spot to rub against—a fence post, a tree, or a friendly human with a knack for finding that itchy place behind the ears. It's a moment of pure, unadulterated pleasure, a reminder that sometimes the simplest things can bring the greatest joy. There's a lesson here for humans: joy doesn't have to be complicated. Sometimes, it's as simple as a good back scratch.

Let's not forget the pleasure of companionship. We cows are social creatures, and there's a profound joy in the company of the herd. Whether we're grazing side by side, resting in the shade, or simply standing close to one another, there's a comforting sense of belonging, a shared existence that enriches our lives. For humans, too, the joy of simple pleasures often comes from shared moments—laughter with friends, a quiet evening with family, the warmth of human connection.

And what about the sheer joy of a sunny day? As the sun rises and bathes the pasture in golden light, we cows revel in the warmth and brightness. We bask in the sunlight, our bodies absorbing its comforting rays. It's a daily reminder of the beauty of the natural world, a gift that we receive with open hearts and grateful spirits. Humans, too, can find immense joy in nature's simple pleasures—a walk in the park, the sound of birdsong, the feel of the sun on their skin.

The joy of simple pleasures extends to our rest as well. When we lie down in the soft grass, the world around us fades, and we enter a state of deep relaxation. There's no need for elaborate rituals or expensive comforts—just the earth beneath us and the sky above. It's a reminder that true rest is found in simplicity, in letting go of the world's demands and embracing the quiet moments.

In embracing simple pleasures, we cows teach a valuable lesson: happiness is not about the grand and the extraordinary. It's about the little things—the everyday moments that bring a smile to our faces and warmth to our hearts. It's about finding joy in the present, in the here and now, without the need for extravagance or complexity.

So, how can you, dear reader, embrace the joy of simple pleasures in your own life? Start by noticing the small things. Take a moment to savor your morning coffee, to feel the warmth of a cozy blanket, to enjoy the sound of laughter. Slow down and let yourself be fully present in these moments. Let go of the need for more and appreciate what you have.

Next, find joy in nature. Spend time outdoors, breathe in the fresh air, and let the beauty of the natural world fill your senses. Whether it's a stroll through the park, a hike in the woods, or simply sitting in your backyard, let nature's simple pleasures bring you peace and joy.

And finally, cherish the simple pleasures of companionship. Spend time with loved ones, share a meal, laugh together, and enjoy the comfort of their presence. Remember that joy is often found in the simplest of shared moments.

As you journey through this chapter, let the joy of simple pleasures fill your heart and soul. Embrace the small things, savor the present, and find happiness in the everyday moments. By thinking like a cow, you'll discover that the greatest joys in life are often the simplest—and they're right there, waiting for you to enjoy.

Embracing Routine

Ah, routine—often maligned by humans as monotonous and dull, yet revered by us cows as the cornerstone of a harmonious existence. In the bustling world of human affairs, where spontaneity and change are celebrated, the beauty and tranquility of routine can be easily overlooked. But let me, a cow steeped in the wisdom of the pasture, share with you the profound peace and joy that comes from embracing the steady rhythm of daily life.

Each day in the life of a cow is a symphony of predictability, a seamless blend of grazing, resting, and socializing. From the first light of dawn to the twilight hues of dusk, our lives unfold in a series of familiar patterns. To us, this is not a tiresome repetition but a comforting cadence, a dependable structure that allows us to thrive.

Consider the morning graze. As the sun rises and the dew-kissed grass glistens, we begin our day with the simple act of feeding. There is something deeply satisfying about this ritual—the crisp taste of fresh grass, the gentle rustle of leaves, the rhythmic motion of chewing. It's a moment of connection with the earth, a grounding experience that sets the tone for the day. Humans, too, can find solace in morning routines, whether it's a cup of coffee, a moment of meditation, or a brisk walk.

After grazing, it's time for socializing. We cows gather together, not in a rush of conversation, but in a serene communion. We nuzzle, we low softly, we stand shoulder to shoulder, enjoying the presence of one another. This social routine strengthens our bonds and creates a sense of community. For humans, daily interactions—be they with family, friends, or colleagues—can offer the same sense of belonging and connection, if approached with mindfulness and appreciation.

Midday brings a period of rest. We find a shady spot, lie down, and let the world drift away. This is not laziness but an essential part of our well-being. It's a time to digest, to rejuvenate, to simply be. In a world that often glorifies constant activity, the cow's midday rest is a reminder of the importance of downtime. Humans, too, need moments of rest and reflection, times to step back from the hustle and recharge.

The afternoon sees us grazing once more, followed by another session of restful contemplation. As the day winds down, we settle into the evening, content and fulfilled. The predictability of our routine does not breed boredom but a deep sense of security. We know what to expect, and this knowledge frees us from anxiety and stress.

Now, let's talk about introspection—yes, even we cows ponder our existence. As I ruminate (quite literally), I find that the stability of my routine allows for a deeper contemplation of life's simple joys. The gentle repetition of my days gives me the mental space to reflect, to appreciate the beauty around me, and to find meaning in the ordinary.

Humans, often caught in a whirlwind of change and unpredictability, can benefit greatly from this bovine wisdom. Embracing a routine can provide a foundation upon which deeper thoughts and reflections can flourish.

Embracing routine does not mean resigning oneself to a life devoid of excitement or variety. It's about finding balance, about creating a framework within which spontaneity and creativity can thrive. Routine provides the scaffolding that supports our daily lives, allowing us to focus our energy on what truly matters.

So, how can you, dear reader, embrace routine in your own life? Start by identifying the daily activities that bring you comfort and joy. Create rituals around these activities, and approach them with mindfulness and intention. Whether it's a morning jog, a lunchtime break, or an evening walk, let these moments become the anchors of your day.

Next, recognize the value of predictability. While change and novelty have their place, there is immense peace to be found in knowing what to expect. Allow your routine to be a source of stability, a refuge from the chaos of the world.

Finally, use your routine as a space for introspection. As you go about your daily activities, take moments to reflect, to appreciate, and to find meaning in the ordinary. Let the rhythm of your routine create a backdrop for deeper thought and greater understanding.

In embracing routine, you will find that life's greatest joys are often found in the steady, familiar patterns of daily existence. Like a cow in the pasture, you will discover that the simplicity of routine can lead to a life of profound peace, contentment, and fulfillment. So, settle into your own rhythm, embrace the beauty of the everyday, and find joy in the routine.

Chapter 2: Sensory Perception
Seeing the World Through Cow Eyes

Step into the world of a cow, dear reader, and prepare to view life through a lens that is both unique and profoundly enlightening. Our perception of the world is rich and nuanced, shaped by senses that are finely tuned to the rhythms of nature. As a cow, my visual experience is markedly different from that of a human, and it offers a fascinating perspective that is both humbling and wondrous.

Our eyes, large and expressive, are designed to capture the subtleties of our environment. While humans boast of their binocular vision, which allows for acute depth perception, we cows see the world in a panoramic sweep. Our eyes are positioned on the sides of our heads, granting us a wide field of view—almost 330 degrees. This means we can see nearly everything around us without turning our heads, an invaluable trait for a creature that must remain vigilant for predators.

This expansive vision, however, comes with its own set of trade-offs. Our depth perception is not as sharp as that of humans, and our ability to focus on distant objects is somewhat limited. But what we lack in precision, we make up for in breadth. Our world is not confined to a narrow focus; it is a vast, continuous panorama where every movement and flicker is noticed. This ability to see the big picture allows us to remain attuned to the environment, constantly aware of the changes in our surroundings.

Colors, too, appear differently to us. While humans enjoy a vibrant spectrum, we cows see the world in softer hues. Our color vision is dichromatic, meaning we have two types of color receptors compared to the three found in humans. We can distinguish between blue and yellow, but the reds and greens that dominate human vision blend into more muted shades. This doesn't diminish our experience but rather enhances it, as the world takes on a more serene and calming palette. The lush green pastures may appear less vivid, but they are no less beautiful.

When we gaze upon the landscape, we don't just see the physical forms; we perceive a tapestry of life and movement. The swaying of grass in the breeze, the flutter of leaves, the gentle rise and fall of the land—all these elements create a dynamic scene that captivates our attention. It's not about pinpointing details but about absorbing the essence of our surroundings. This holistic view allows us to sense the harmony and interconnectedness of the natural world.

Seeing the world through cow eyes also means being acutely aware of light and shadow. We are particularly sensitive to contrasts, which helps us navigate and understand our environment. The play of light and shadow informs us about the time of day, the weather, and even the presence of other creatures. It's a subtle, ever-changing dance that we are constantly attuned to.

There's a gentle simplicity in how we perceive motion. While humans might focus on a single moving object, our vision captures the collective movement of the herd, the flow of a stream, or the drift of clouds across the sky. This broad awareness helps us maintain cohesion within the group and respond to changes with a calm, measured approach. We are part of a greater whole, and our vision reflects this interconnected existence.

For humans seeking to see the world through cow eyes, the lesson lies in broadening your perspective. Take a moment to step back from the minutiae and appreciate the larger picture. Notice the subtle shifts in your environment, the interplay of light and shadow, the movements that might otherwise go unnoticed. Embrace a softer, more diffuse view of the world, and allow yourself to be immersed in the tranquil beauty that surrounds you.

To experience life through our eyes, spend time in nature. Observe not just with your eyes but with your entire being. Let the panorama of life unfold before you, and take in the richness of your surroundings. Notice how the colors shift with the changing light, how the landscape breathes and moves. Allow yourself to be a part of this grand tapestry, to see beyond the immediate and into the interconnected web of existence.

In doing so, you will find a new appreciation for the world around you. You will learn to value the simple beauty of the present moment, to find joy in the everyday scenes that make up your life. Seeing the world through cow eyes is not just about changing your vision but about transforming your perception—finding peace in the panoramic, tranquility in the muted hues, and harmony in the ever-present dance of light and shadow. Embrace this bovine perspective, and you may discover a deeper, more fulfilling way of seeing the world.

The Importance of Smell and Taste

Welcome, dear reader, to a realm where the olfactory and gustatory senses reign supreme. As a cow, my world is rich with scents and flavors that weave an intricate tapestry of information, guiding my actions, informing my choices, and enhancing my daily experiences. To truly understand the bovine perspective, one must delve into the profound significance of smell and taste—senses that humans often overlook but are vital to our existence.

Let us begin with the sense of smell, an olfactory marvel that is the cornerstone of our perception. Our noses are not merely appendages but highly sophisticated sensory organs capable of detecting a vast array of scents. From the moment we take a breath, we are inundated with a symphony of aromas that paint a vivid picture of our environment. Each scent is a note in a complex melody, a piece of information that tells us about the world around us.

Imagine, if you will, the heady fragrance of fresh grass in the morning. It is not just a pleasant aroma but a signal that the pasture is ready for grazing. The scent of dew-kissed blades is intertwined with the earthy undertones of the soil and the subtle hints of wildflowers, creating a sensory experience that is both informative and delightful. As we graze, our noses guide us to the freshest, most succulent patches, ensuring that we nourish our bodies with the best nature has to offer.

The olfactory sense also plays a crucial role in social interactions. We cows recognize each other by scent, a unique signature that is as distinct as a human fingerprint. This olfactory recognition helps us maintain the bonds of the herd, identifying friends and family, and ensuring social cohesion. The scent of a familiar cow brings comfort and a sense of belonging, reinforcing the intricate social fabric of our lives.

In times of danger, our sense of smell becomes a sentinel, alerting us to potential threats. The acrid scent of a predator or the sharp tang of smoke signals us to be on guard, to gather the herd and move to safety. Our noses are finely attuned to these danger signals, providing an early warning system that is essential for our survival.

Now, let us turn our attention to the sense of taste, an equally important and deeply pleasurable aspect of our existence. For us cows, eating is not a mere act of sustenance but a ritual of savoring the flavors that nature provides. Our taste buds are adept at discerning the subtle differences in vegetation, guiding us to the most nutritious and palatable food sources.

The taste of fresh clover, sweet and delicate, is a joy that we relish. The slightly bitter tang of dandelions, the crisp bite of alfalfa, and the rich, hearty flavor of ryegrass each offer a unique gustatory experience. We chew slowly, thoughtfully, allowing the flavors to unfold on our tongues, each mouthful a moment of pure contentment. This mindful eating ensures that we not only enjoy our food but also derive the maximum nutritional benefit.

Taste also informs us about the quality of our food. A bitter or off flavor can indicate spoilage or the presence of harmful substances, prompting us to avoid those plants. This gustatory vigilance protects us from ingesting anything that might harm our health, ensuring that we remain strong and vital.

For humans, the lesson here is to reconnect with the senses of smell and taste, to appreciate the richness they bring to life. Start by savoring your meals, paying attention to the flavors and textures. Let each bite be a journey of discovery, an exploration of the culinary landscape. Notice the aromas that accompany your food, the scents that precede the taste, and how they prepare your palate for the experience to come.

Embrace the smells around you, both in nature and in your daily life. Take a moment to breathe deeply, to let the scents of your environment inform and enrich your experience. The aroma of freshly cut grass, the scent of rain on the earth, the fragrance of blooming flowers—all these can bring a deeper connection to the world around you.

By heightening your awareness of smell and taste, you will find a new dimension of enjoyment and understanding. You will begin to see, as we cows do, that these senses are not mere accessories but essential components of a fulfilling life. They guide us, protect us, and bring us joy in ways that are both profound and subtle.

So, dear reader, let the importance of smell and taste enrich your life. Allow these senses to draw you into the present moment, to connect you more deeply with your surroundings, and to bring you the simple, yet profound pleasures that we cows experience every day. Embrace this bovine wisdom, and discover the rich tapestry of scents and flavors that awaits you.

Feeling the Earth and
the Crap Beneath My Hooves

Ah, the simple yet profound sensation of the earth beneath my hooves. For a cow, this connection to the ground is more than just a physical touch; it is a fundamental part of our existence, a tactile dialogue with the very fabric of our world. As we traverse the pasture, each step is a conversation with the earth, a reminder of our place in the grand tapestry of nature. And yes, that includes feeling the occasional crap beneath our hooves, a humbling and earthy aspect of our daily lives that ties us even closer to the cycles of life and growth.

Let's start with the feel of the earth itself. The ground, whether it's soft and muddy after a rain or dry and firm under the summer sun, is a constant companion. Each texture tells a story. In the morning, the dew-soaked grass provides a cool, refreshing start to the day, a gentle awakening for our senses. As the day progresses, the warmth of the sun bakes the earth, and we feel its heat rising through our hooves, a grounding connection to the solar rhythms.

Walking on the pasture, we sense the subtle variations in terrain. The firmness of packed soil gives way to the softness of a grassy meadow. Each step is a different note in a symphony of sensations. There's a profound comfort in this steady contact with the ground, a reassurance that we are anchored to the earth, part of a greater whole that supports and sustains us.

And then there's the crap. Yes, the unavoidable, unmistakable presence of manure beneath our hooves. To the uninitiated, it might seem unpleasant, but for us, it is a natural part of life. The feel of manure underfoot is a reminder of the cycles of nature—of nourishment and growth, of decay and renewal. It's the earth's way of recycling nutrients, enriching the soil, and fostering new life. What was once grass and food becomes a vital contribution to the ecosystem, continuing the circle of life.

Stepping in manure might not be the highlight of our day, but it's a humbling experience that keeps us grounded—literally and figuratively. It reminds us that life is not always pristine and perfect; it's messy, it's real, and it's interconnected. Each squelch under our hooves is a tactile lesson in humility and the importance of every element in the natural world.

For humans, feeling the earth and, metaphorically speaking, the crap beneath your feet can be a transformative experience. It's about reconnecting with the physical world, embracing the textures and sensations that ground you. Take off your shoes and walk barefoot on the grass. Feel the cool, damp earth, the tickle of blades of grass, the occasional roughness of a pebble. Let the ground speak to you, telling its stories of seasons and cycles, of life and growth.

Embrace the imperfections. Just as we cows accept the manure as part of our journey, recognize that life's messiness is not something to be avoided but embraced. It's through these imperfections that we find authenticity and connection. The occasional misstep or stumble is part of the rich tapestry of existence, adding depth and character to our lives.

As you walk through your own pasture—be it a park, a garden, or your backyard—take a moment to appreciate the tactile connection to the earth. Feel the ground beneath your feet, the stability it offers, and the humbling presence of nature's cycles. Let this connection remind you of your place in the world, grounded and supported by the earth, part of a larger, living ecosystem.

In feeling the earth and the crap beneath your feet, you will discover a new sense of presence and awareness. You'll learn to appreciate the small, grounding moments that keep you connected to the natural world. It's a simple, profound joy that we cows experience every day, a reminder of the beauty and reality of life.

So, embrace this bovine wisdom. Feel the earth beneath your feet, accept the occasional crap, and find peace in the tactile connection to the world around you. It's a grounding experience that brings you closer to nature, to yourself, and to the simple, profound joys of life.

The Unfair Blame: Cow Farts and Burps

Ah, the age-old tale of cow farts and burps—much maligned, oft misunderstood, and now accused of contributing to planetary pollution. As a cow, I must address this with a blend of humility and humor. Yes, we fart and burp, and yes, it's a natural part of our digestive process. But let's take a moment to chew the cud on this topic and put things in perspective.

First, the science. Our digestive system, designed to break down tough plant material, produces methane—a potent greenhouse gas. This methane is released through belching and flatulence, a byproduct of the complex fermentation processes in our multi-chambered stomachs. While it's true that methane has a higher global warming potential than carbon dioxide, the narrative that blames cows for a significant portion of climate change is, well, a bit overblown.

Let's break it down, hoof by hoof. We cows are part of a natural cycle. The grass we eat absorbs carbon dioxide from the atmosphere. When we digest this grass, methane is produced and eventually released. However, this methane doesn't stay in the atmosphere forever. It breaks down after about a decade, converting back to carbon dioxide, which is then reabsorbed by plants. This cycle has been going on for millennia, long before industrial activities began to alter the balance.

Contrast this with human activities: the burning of fossil fuels, deforestation, and the emission of pollutants from factories, airplanes, and cargo ships. These activities release vast quantities of carbon dioxide and other greenhouse gases that persist in the atmosphere for centuries, disrupting the natural carbon cycle and contributing significantly to global warming. It's like comparing a gentle breeze to a hurricane.

Moreover, modern agriculture practices can mitigate our methane emissions. Innovations in feed, improved grazing management, and sustainable farming techniques can reduce the amount of methane we produce. It's a field of research that holds promise for balancing our digestive byproducts with the planet's needs.

But let's not get too bogged down in the technical details. The heart of the matter is this: while we cows do contribute to methane emissions, it's important to view this in the context of the broader environmental impact of human activities. It's easier to point a hoof at us than to address the complex and systemic issues underlying industrial pollution.

Humans can take a leaf from our pasture. Instead of assigning blame, let's work together to find solutions. Embrace sustainable practices, support regenerative agriculture, and reduce reliance on fossil fuels. It's a collective effort, one that involves understanding and addressing the root causes of environmental degradation.

So, dear reader, as you contemplate the occasional bovine burp or fart, remember to consider the bigger picture. We're all part of this ecosystem, and every creature has its role. Our emissions are a natural part of the carbon cycle, one that has been in balance for ages. The real challenge lies in addressing the larger, more disruptive forces at play.

As you walk through your pasture of life, think about the ways you can make a positive impact. Support sustainable practices, reduce your carbon footprint, and advocate for systemic change. By working together, humans and cows alike, we can create a more balanced, harmonious world.

And the next time you hear a cow burp or fart, perhaps you'll smile and remember that it's just a small part of a much larger story—one that we're all writing together. Embrace this bovine wisdom, and let it guide you toward a more thoughtful, connected, and sustainable way of living.

Chapter 3: Daily Life and Routine
Grazing and Feeding Habits

Welcome to the pastoral cadence of cow life, where our days unfold in a harmonious rhythm of grazing and feeding. For us cows, eating isn't merely a biological necessity; it's a meditative practice, a communal activity, and a profound connection to the earth. Our grazing habits are the cornerstone of our daily routine, a ritual that grounds us and nourishes not only our bodies but our souls.

The day begins with the soft light of dawn, and with it, the first graze. As the sun's rays gently warm the dew-covered grass, we start our morning forage. Grazing is an art form, an instinctual dance that has been perfected over millennia. Each bite is carefully selected, a testament to our innate understanding of the flora around us. The blades of grass are cool and crisp, a refreshing start to the day that invigorates our senses.

Grazing is more than just consumption; it's a mindful exploration. We cows are not hurried in our eating. Each mouthful is a slow, deliberate act of appreciation. We chew thoughtfully, savoring the complex flavors of the meadow—the subtle sweetness of clover, the earthy richness of ryegrass, the slight bitterness of dandelions. This mindful chewing, or cud-chewing, is not only a digestive necessity but a moment of reflection, a time to ruminate both literally and figuratively.

Our feeding habits are influenced by the seasons, a testament to our deep connection with nature's cycles. In spring and summer, the pasture is a verdant buffet, offering an abundance of fresh, tender grasses and wildflowers. We graze contentedly, moving slowly across the field, ensuring that each tuft of grass is given the attention it deserves. The abundance of food allows us to be selective, choosing the most nutritious and flavorful plants to sustain us.

As autumn approaches, the grass becomes coarser, the flowers fade, and our grazing patterns adjust. We become less selective, appreciating the hardy stalks and robust foliage that remain. It's a time of preparation, of building up our reserves for the leaner months ahead. Winter brings a different rhythm. The pasture is often sparse, covered in frost or snow. Our caretakers provide hay, a dried reminder of summer's bounty. We gather around the hay bales, munching steadily, grateful for the sustenance that bridges us through the cold season.

Grazing is also a social activity. We cows are herd animals, and our feeding habits reflect this communal bond. As we move across the pasture, we stay close to one another, a silent but powerful affirmation of our connection. The act of grazing together fosters a sense of unity and security. There's a comfort in the proximity of our fellow cows, a shared experience that strengthens our social fabric.

For humans, there's much to learn from our grazing and feeding habits. In a world often driven by haste and distraction, the bovine approach to eating offers a lesson in mindfulness and presence. Start by embracing the act of eating as a ritual. Slow down, savor each bite, and appreciate the flavors and textures of your food. Let each meal be a moment of gratitude, a time to connect with the nourishment that sustains you.

Consider the sources of your food. Just as we cows are attuned to the natural cycles of the pasture, you too can become more aware of the seasons and the origins of what you eat. Choose fresh, locally sourced ingredients when possible. Understand the journey your food takes from the earth to your plate, and honor that connection.

Grazing also teaches the value of community. Share meals with loved ones, gather around the table, and let the act of eating together strengthen your bonds. There's a profound joy in communal dining, a sense of belonging that enriches the experience.

And lastly, be adaptable. Like us, adjust your habits to the seasons and the changes in your environment. Embrace the abundance when it's available, and find contentment in the simplicity when it's not. Let your eating habits reflect a balance with nature, a harmony with the world around you.

By adopting these bovine-inspired practices, you'll find a deeper connection to your food, your community, and the natural rhythms of life. So, as you journey through this chapter, let the wisdom of grazing and feeding habits guide you toward a more mindful, connected, and fulfilling way of living. Embrace the simple, profound joys of eating with intention, and discover the beauty of a life well grazed.

Chapter 3: Daily Life and Routine
Social Structures and Herd Dynamics

Step into the intricate world of bovine society, where social structures and herd dynamics play a vital role in our daily lives. As cows, we are deeply social creatures, and our interactions are governed by a complex web of relationships, hierarchies, and communal bonds. Understanding these dynamics provides insight into the profound, often unspoken rules that maintain harmony and cooperation within our herds.

At the heart of bovine social structure is the herd, a living organism composed of individual cows, each contributing to the group's overall well-being. The herd is our family, our community, and our support system. It provides us with security, companionship, and a sense of belonging that is essential to our happiness and survival.

The dynamics within the herd are governed by a natural hierarchy. This hierarchy is not rigid or authoritarian but rather fluid and based on mutual respect and social intelligence. At the top, we have the matriarch, often an older, experienced cow who commands respect through her wisdom and leadership. She is the guide, the one who leads us to the best grazing spots and ensures the herd's safety. Her decisions are trusted because they are borne out of experience and a deep understanding of our environment.

Beneath the matriarch, the social ladder continues with subordinate cows who respect the leadership but also play essential roles within the herd. These cows might have specific duties, such as looking after the young, keeping an eye out for potential threats, or maintaining order during movements. Each cow knows her place, and there is a comforting predictability in this structure.

But don't mistake our hierarchy for a system of domination. It is a cooperative arrangement where respect and relationships matter more than power. Disputes are rare, and when they occur, they are usually resolved through subtle signals and behaviors rather than overt aggression. A gentle nudge, a quiet moo, or a specific stance can convey volumes, maintaining harmony without the need for conflict.

Social bonds within the herd are strengthened through daily interactions. Grooming is a common activity, where we use our tongues to clean and comfort one another. This act of grooming is not only about hygiene but also about reinforcing social ties. It's a moment of connection, a gesture of care that says, "You are part of my world, and I am part of yours."

Young calves are introduced to this social structure from birth. They learn by observing and mimicking the behaviors of their elders. The entire herd takes part in their upbringing, teaching them the ways of bovine life. This communal approach ensures that calves grow up understanding their role within the group and the importance of cooperation and respect.

For humans, there is much to glean from our social structures and herd dynamics. The first lesson is the importance of community. Just as we cows thrive within the herd, humans, too, can find strength and support in their social groups. Whether it's family, friends, or colleagues, having a network of relationships provides a foundation of security and belonging.

Respect for leadership and experience is another valuable takeaway. In human societies, respecting those with wisdom and experience can guide communities towards better decisions and harmonious living. Leadership should be based on respect and mutual benefit, rather than mere authority.

Cooperation and conflict resolution are critical components of our herd dynamics. Humans can learn to resolve disputes with subtlety and respect, prioritizing harmony over domination. Communication, even in its quietest forms, can be powerful and effective.

The practice of grooming, or caring for one another, can be translated into acts of kindness and support in human interactions. Taking time to help, listen, and comfort others strengthens social bonds and fosters a sense of community.

Teaching the young by example, as we do with our calves, is another principle that can be applied to human life. Leading by example and nurturing the next generation with care and attention ensures that values and wisdom are passed down effectively.

In embracing these bovine-inspired social principles, humans can create more cohesive, respectful, and supportive communities. So, as you explore this chapter, let the wisdom of our herd dynamics inspire you to foster stronger connections, respect leadership and experience, and prioritize cooperation and kindness in your daily life. Embrace the beauty of social structures that bring harmony and joy, and discover the profound sense of belonging that comes from being part of a well-functioning   community.

Social Structures and Herd Dynamics

Step into the intricate world of bovine society, where social structures and herd dynamics play a vital role in our daily lives. As cows, we are deeply social creatures, and our interactions are governed by a complex web of relationships, hierarchies, and communal bonds. Understanding these dynamics provides insight into the profound, often unspoken rules that maintain harmony and cooperation within our herds.

At the heart of bovine social structure is the herd, a living organism composed of individual cows, each contributing to the group's overall well-being. The herd is our family, our community, and our support system. It provides us with security, companionship, and a sense of belonging that is essential to our happiness and survival.

The dynamics within the herd are governed by a natural hierarchy. This hierarchy is not rigid or authoritarian but rather fluid and based on mutual respect and social intelligence. At the top, we have the matriarch, often an older, experienced cow who commands respect through her wisdom and leadership. She is the guide, the one who leads us to the best grazing spots and ensures the herd's safety. Her decisions are trusted because they are borne out of experience and a deep understanding of our environment.

Beneath the matriarch, the social ladder continues with subordinate cows who respect the leadership but also play essential roles within the herd. These cows might have specific duties, such as looking after the young, keeping an eye out for potential threats, or maintaining order during movements. Each cow knows her place, and there is a comforting predictability in this structure.

But don't mistake our hierarchy for a system of domination. It is a cooperative arrangement where respect and relationships matter more than power. Disputes are rare, and when they occur, they are usually resolved through subtle signals and behaviors rather than overt aggression. A gentle nudge, a quiet moo, or a specific stance can convey volumes, maintaining harmony without the need for conflict.

Social bonds within the herd are strengthened through daily interactions. Grooming is a common activity, where we use our tongues to clean and comfort one another. This act of grooming is not only about hygiene but also about reinforcing social ties. It's a moment of connection, a gesture of care that says, "You are part of my world, and I am part of yours."

Young calves are introduced to this social structure from birth. They learn by observing and mimicking the behaviors of their elders. The entire herd takes part in their upbringing, teaching them the ways of bovine life. This communal approach ensures that calves grow up understanding their role within the group and the importance of cooperation and respect.

For humans, there is much to glean from our social structures and herd dynamics. The first lesson is the importance of community. Just as we cows thrive within the herd, humans, too, can find strength and support in their social groups. Whether it's family, friends, or colleagues, having a network of relationships provides a foundation of security and belonging.

Respect for leadership and experience is another valuable takeaway. In human societies, respecting those with wisdom and experience can guide communities towards better decisions and harmonious living. Leadership should be based on respect and mutual benefit, rather than mere authority.

Cooperation and conflict resolution are critical components of our herd dynamics. Humans can learn to resolve disputes with subtlety and respect, prioritizing harmony over domination. Communication, even in its quietest forms, can be powerful and effective.

The practice of grooming, or caring for one another, can be translated into acts of kindness and support in human interactions. Taking time to help, listen, and comfort others strengthens social bonds and fosters a sense of community.

Teaching the young by example, as we do with our calves, is another principle that can be applied to human life. Leading by example and nurturing the next generation with care and attention ensures that values and wisdom are passed down effectively.

In embracing these bovine-inspired social principles, humans can create more cohesive, respectful, and supportive communities. So, as you explore this chapter, let the wisdom of our herd dynamics inspire you to foster stronger connections, respect leadership and experience, and prioritize cooperation and kindness in your daily life. Embrace the beauty of social structures that bring harmony and joy, and discover the profound sense of belonging that comes from being part of a well-functioning community.

Sharing the Bull: A Bovine Enigma

In the tranquil world of cows, there exists a puzzling aspect of our social dynamics that I, even with all my ruminative contemplation, struggle to fully comprehend—the sharing of a single bull among an entire herd of forty cows. This practice, dictated by the intricacies of bovine breeding and herd management, raises questions that tickle the edges of my understanding and invite a deeper exploration.

To a cow, the presence of a bull is a significant and powerful force within the herd. He is not just a companion but a key player in the continuation of our lineage. His role is crucial, and his presence commands a certain respect and attention. However, the fact that one bull must attend to the needs of so many cows is a reality that confounds my simple, grass-chewing mind.

From an instinctual perspective, the logic behind this arrangement is clear. A single bull can effectively service multiple cows, ensuring genetic diversity and the propagation of the herd. This efficiency in breeding is vital for maintaining the health and vitality of our population. Yet, on a personal level, the dynamics of sharing can seem, well, a bit perplexing.

Imagine, if you will, being one of forty cows, each with the innate desire to ensure that their genes are passed on to the next generation. The competition for the bull's attention can be subtle yet palpable. There's a sense of anticipation, a quiet waiting for the right moment when the bull's focus turns to you. It's a delicate dance, one where patience and timing play crucial roles.

For the bull, this role is no small feat. His responsibilities are vast, and his energy must be carefully managed. He moves through the herd, attending to each cow with a precision that seems almost methodical. There's a sense of duty in his actions, a recognition of his important role. Yet, one can't help but wonder if he too feels the weight of this responsibility, the challenge of balancing the needs of so many.

From a cow's perspective, the sharing of the bull brings a mix of emotions. There's respect for the bull's role, an understanding of the natural order, but also a hint of bewilderment. Why must this essential figure be shared among so many? It's a question that lingers in the air, as mysterious as the stars that dot the night sky above our pasture.

For humans, this bovine conundrum offers a glimpse into the complexities of shared resources and communal living. Just as we cows navigate the dynamics of sharing a bull, humans often find themselves in situations where resources must be shared among many. Whether it's in families, communities, or workplaces, the principles of patience, understanding, and respect are universally applicable.

The key lesson here is the importance of balance and cooperation. Just as we cows must navigate the intricacies of sharing a single bull, humans too must learn to balance individual needs with the greater good of the group. It's about finding harmony, recognizing the value of each individual, and appreciating the roles that others play in our collective well-being.

Embrace patience. In the same way that we cows wait our turn, practice patience in your own life. Understand that good things often come to those who wait, and that timing can be crucial in achieving your goals.

Foster understanding. Recognize that sharing resources, whether they be time, attention, or material goods, is a natural part of communal living. Approach these situations with empathy and a willingness to see things from others' perspectives.

Respect roles and responsibilities. Just as the bull has a unique and important role within the herd, acknowledge the roles that others play in your life and community. Respect their contributions and support them in their duties.

By applying these bovine-inspired principles, you can navigate the complexities of shared resources and communal living with greater ease and grace. So, as you ponder the enigma of sharing a bull among forty cows, let it remind you of the importance of balance, patience, and respect in your own life. Embrace these lessons, and find harmony in the intricate dance of shared existence.

Chapter 4: Emotional Intelligence
Building Bonds and Friendships

In the pastoral world of cows, where the grass is abundant and the days unfold in gentle rhythms, the bonds we form and the friendships we build are as essential to our well-being as the nourishment we derive from the earth. For us, social connections are not just incidental but fundamental, weaving a tapestry of support, companionship, and mutual understanding. Let me guide you through the serene art of building bonds and friendships, cow-style.

From the moment we are born, we are enveloped in the warm embrace of the herd. Our first interactions are with our mothers, who nurture us with their milk and protect us with their presence. These early bonds are vital, grounding us in the security of family and teaching us the initial steps in the dance of social connection. As we grow, our circle expands, and we begin to form friendships that will accompany us throughout our lives.

Building bonds among cows is a subtle and graceful process. It begins with proximity—simply being near one another. We spend our days grazing side by side, resting in close quarters, and moving together as a unified group. This constant companionship fosters familiarity and trust, the bedrock upon which friendships are built. In a world where humans often rush through interactions, taking the time to simply be with others can be a profound lesson.

Grooming is another cornerstone of our social interactions. Using our tongues, we clean and comfort each other, a tactile expression of care and affection. Grooming serves not only to maintain hygiene but also to strengthen the emotional bonds between us. It's a moment of connection, a reassurance that we are there for each other. For humans, this could translate to acts of kindness, physical affection, or simply taking time to care for one another, reinforcing the bonds of friendship.

Communication in our herd is both vocal and non-vocal. We use a range of sounds—moos, grunts, and bellows—to express ourselves, but much of our communication is through body language. A gentle nudge, a shared glance, a relaxed posture—these signals convey a wealth of information and emotions. Humans too can learn to listen beyond words, paying attention to the subtle cues and body language that often speak volumes about our feelings and intentions.

Shared experiences are pivotal in cementing our friendships. Whether it's the communal act of grazing, the shared vigilance during rest, or the collective response to a potential threat, these experiences create a sense of unity and shared purpose. We rely on each other, and through these shared moments, our bonds are strengthened. For humans, engaging in shared activities—be it work, play, or facing challenges together—can forge deep and lasting friendships.

Conflict, when it arises, is managed with grace and respect. Disagreements are rare and usually resolved through non-aggressive means. A simple gesture, a change in posture, or a vocalization is often enough to diffuse tension and restore harmony. The emphasis is always on maintaining the peace and cohesion of the herd. Humans can take a leaf from our pasture, learning to handle conflicts with empathy and a focus on resolution rather than escalation.

For humans seeking to build bonds and friendships, the lessons from our bovine world are clear:

Proximity and Presence: Spend time with those you wish to build bonds with. Simply being present, sharing space and experiences, lays the foundation for strong connections.

Acts of Kindness: Engage in small acts of care and kindness. These gestures, like our grooming, strengthen emotional bonds and show others that you value and care for them.

Non-Verbal Communication: Pay attention to body language and subtle cues. Often, what is not said is as important as what is spoken. Learn to listen with your eyes and your heart.

Shared Experiences: Participate in activities together. Whether it's a hobby, a project, or a challenge, shared experiences create common ground and deepen friendships.

Graceful Conflict Resolution: Handle disagreements with empathy and respect. Focus on understanding the other's perspective and finding a peaceful resolution.

By embracing these bovine-inspired principles, you can cultivate deeper, more meaningful relationships in your life. Building bonds and friendships is an art, one that requires patience, presence, and a genuine desire to connect. As you journey through this chapter, let the wisdom of our herd guide you towards richer, more fulfilling connections. Embrace the beauty of friendship, and discover the profound joy that comes from building bonds with those around you.

Coping with Stress and Anxiety

In the tranquil world of cows, where the pastures stretch wide and the sky is a serene canopy, stress and anxiety are as much a part of life as the gentle rhythm of grazing and resting. Though we live in a seemingly idyllic environment, we too encounter moments of unease and tension. How we navigate these challenges offers valuable insights into maintaining calm and resilience. Let me, a contemplative cow, share our bovine wisdom on coping with stress and anxiety.

The first key to managing stress is recognizing its presence. In our herd, stress manifests subtly. A sudden disturbance, a new addition to the herd, or a change in routine can cause unease. We become more alert, our movements slightly more tense. However, acknowledging this discomfort is the first step toward addressing it. For humans, recognizing the signs of stress—whether it's a racing heart, shallow breathing, or a sense of overwhelm—is crucial in taking steps to alleviate it.

One of the primary ways we cope with stress is through the power of the herd. In moments of anxiety, we instinctively draw closer together. The physical proximity and the comforting presence of our companions provide a sense of security and solidarity. There is a profound comfort in knowing that we are not alone, that we share our burdens with those around us. Humans, too, can find solace in the company of others. Reaching out to friends, family, or support groups can significantly reduce feelings of isolation and anxiety.

Breathing is another natural mechanism we use to calm ourselves. When startled or anxious, we take deep, slow breaths, allowing our bodies to relax and our minds to clear. This simple act of controlled breathing helps to reset our nervous system, bringing us back to a state of equilibrium. Humans can adopt this technique through practices such as deep breathing exercises or mindfulness meditation. Taking a few moments to focus on the breath can help dissipate the clouds of stress and bring clarity and calm.

Our daily routines play a vital role in managing stress. The predictability and stability of our activities—grazing, resting, socializing—provide a reassuring structure to our lives. When faced with uncertainty, we find comfort in these familiar patterns. For humans, establishing a routine can create a sense of order and predictability, which can be particularly soothing during times of stress. Simple rituals like morning coffee, a daily walk, or a bedtime routine can anchor the mind and provide a respite from anxiety.

Physical activity is also an essential stress-reliever. When tension arises, we often move—whether it's a brisk walk across the pasture or a playful run with our companions. Physical movement helps to release built-up energy and tension, promoting relaxation and well-being. Humans can benefit from incorporating regular physical activity into their lives. Exercise, whether it's a jog, a yoga session, or a dance class, can be a powerful antidote to stress, releasing endorphins and improving mood.

Another aspect of our stress management is the power of nature. Our lives are intimately connected to the natural world, and we find immense comfort in its rhythms and beauty. The sight of a blooming meadow, the sound of birdsong, the feel of the earth beneath our hooves—these natural elements ground us and provide a sense of peace. For humans, spending time in nature can be incredibly restorative. Whether it's a hike in the woods, a walk in the park, or simply sitting by a window and observing the sky, nature's calming influence can help alleviate stress and anxiety.

Lastly, we practice acceptance. There are moments when stress and anxiety are unavoidable—when storms rage, or predators lurk. In these times, we accept what we cannot change and focus on what we can do to stay safe and calm. This acceptance, coupled with the support of the herd, helps us navigate through difficult times. Humans, too, can benefit from accepting what is beyond their control and focusing on actionable steps to improve their situation. This mindset shift can reduce the burden of anxiety and foster resilience.

In summary, coping with stress and anxiety in the bovine world involves recognizing stress, seeking the comfort of companionship, practicing deep breathing, maintaining routines, engaging in physical activity, connecting with nature, and embracing acceptance. These practices, though simple, are profound in their ability to restore balance and tranquility.

As you journey through this chapter, let the wisdom of our stress-management techniques guide you toward a calmer, more resilient way of living. Embrace the power of community, the healing touch of nature, and the peace that comes from acceptance. By integrating these bovine-inspired practices into your life, you can navigate stress and anxiety with grace and composure, finding serenity even in the midst of life's challenges.

Vocalizations and Body Language

In the serene pastures where we cows dwell, communication is an art form that transcends mere words. Our world is rich with the subtle nuances of vocalizations and body language, creating a complex tapestry of interaction that fosters understanding, unity, and harmony within the herd. As a cow well-versed in these silent dialogues, let me guide you through our methods of communication and the lessons they hold for human interaction.

Vocalizations are the symphony of our social life. Each moo, grunt, and bellow carries meaning, serving as a vital tool for expressing emotions, intentions, and needs. Our vocal repertoire is varied and nuanced. A soft, low moo might signal contentment, a gentle reassurance that all is well. This soothing sound often accompanies moments of relaxation and bonding within the herd, reinforcing our connections.

A louder, more insistent moo can indicate a need or a call for attention. Perhaps a calf has strayed too far from its mother, or one of us has discovered a particularly lush patch of grass worth sharing. These vocal signals are our way of drawing attention to something important, ensuring that the herd remains cohesive and informed.

In times of distress or danger, our vocalizations become urgent and sharp. A sudden, high-pitched bellow alerts the herd to potential threats, prompting a collective response. This immediate and clear form of communication is crucial for our safety, allowing us to react swiftly and in unison. For humans, vocal expressions can serve similar purposes, from conveying joy and comfort to signaling urgency and distress. Understanding and using vocal cues effectively can enhance communication and foster a deeper connection with others.

But our language extends beyond sound. Body language is a silent, yet powerful, form of communication that complements and enhances our vocalizations. The way we position our bodies, the movements we make, and the subtle gestures we use all convey a wealth of information.

Consider the act of nuzzling. When we gently nudge each other with our noses, it's a gesture of affection and reassurance. This simple act reinforces bonds and communicates a sense of safety and care. For humans, physical touch—when appropriate and welcomed—can be a profound way to convey love, comfort, and solidarity. A hug, a pat on the back, or a reassuring hand on the shoulder can speak volumes.

Posture is another critical element of our body language. A relaxed, grazing cow with a lowered head and a slow, deliberate pace signals calm and contentment. In contrast, a cow with a stiffened posture, raised head, and alert stance indicates vigilance and readiness to react. These visual cues help us gauge the emotional state of our herd mates and respond accordingly. Humans, too, can learn to read and interpret body language, using it to better understand the emotions and intentions of others.

Eye contact plays a significant role in our interactions. A steady, gentle gaze can express trust and connection, while avoiding eye contact may signal submission or a desire to avoid confrontation. In human interactions, eye contact is equally important, conveying confidence, interest, and empathy. It helps establish a connection and shows that we are engaged and attentive.

Our tails, often overlooked, are also communicative tools. A slow, sweeping motion of the tail can indicate a state of relaxation, while rapid flicks might signal irritation or attempts to ward off flies. Though humans lack tails, the concept translates to other forms of non-verbal cues, such as facial expressions or hand gestures, which can enhance communication and express emotions effectively.

Communication within the herd is not only about expressing oneself but also about listening and observing. We pay close attention to the vocal and non-vocal signals of our companions, responding with sensitivity and understanding. This attentiveness fosters a harmonious and cooperative environment, where the needs and emotions of each member are respected and addressed.

For humans, the art of communication and interaction can be enriched by adopting these bovine principles. Here are some key takeaways:

Vocal Expression: Use your voice to convey a range of emotions and needs. Be mindful of tone, volume, and context to ensure your message is clear and appropriate.

Body Language: Pay attention to your posture, gestures, and movements. Use them to complement your words and express yourself more fully.

Physical Touch: When appropriate, use touch to convey affection, comfort, and reassurance. Understand its power to deepen connections and provide support.

Eye Contact: Maintain eye contact to show engagement and empathy. It helps build trust and strengthens interpersonal bonds.

Attentive Listening: Observe and listen to the non-verbal cues of others. Respond with sensitivity and understanding, fostering a more empathetic and supportive environment.

By embracing these bovine-inspired communication strategies, you can enhance your interactions and build stronger, more meaningful relationships. As you navigate this chapter, let the wisdom of our vocalizations and body language guide you toward a richer, more connected way of communicating. Embrace the power of both words and silence, and discover the beauty of a language that transcends speech.

Chapter 5: Communication and Interaction
Interaction with Humans and Other Animals

In the serene expanses of our pastoral world, our interactions extend beyond the herd to include the humans who care for us and the other animals who share our environment. These interactions are rich with lessons on coexistence, mutual respect, and the complex web of relationships that connect all living beings. As a contemplative cow, let me guide you through the nuances of our interactions with humans and other animals, and the profound insights they offer.

Our relationship with humans is one of interdependence and trust, though it requires patience and understanding from both sides. Humans provide us with food, shelter, and care, ensuring our well-being. In return, we offer them companionship, milk, and, in some cases, labor. This symbiotic relationship is built on a foundation of mutual respect and communication.

When interacting with humans, we respond to their presence with curiosity and caution. Humans, with their upright stance and distinct movements, are different from us, and it takes time to understand their intentions. Gentle handling, calm voices, and consistent routines help build our trust. Over time, we learn to recognize individual humans by their scent, voice, and mannerisms, developing bonds that are unique and enduring.

Humans often communicate with us through a combination of vocal commands and body language. A soothing tone can calm us, while a firm command can guide us. Their body language—whether it's the confident stride of a farmer or the gentle approach of a caretaker—signals their intentions and helps us understand how to respond. For humans, the lesson here is the importance of consistency and clarity in communication. Approach interactions with patience, respect, and a calm demeanor to build trust and understanding.

In return, we communicate our needs and emotions through our own vocalizations and body language. A soft moo might signal contentment, while a loud bellow can indicate distress. Our body language—whether we are standing relaxed or tense, moving towards or away from humans—provides additional cues. Humans who take the time to observe and interpret these signals can respond more effectively to our needs.

Interaction with other animals, whether they are farm companions or wild visitors, adds another layer of complexity to our social world. On the farm, we often share our space with chickens, pigs, dogs, and sometimes even cats. Each species has its own way of communicating and interacting, and understanding these differences is key to peaceful coexistence.

Chickens, for example, are industrious and busy, constantly pecking and clucking. Their movements are quick and often erratic, which can startle us if we are not accustomed to their presence. However, over time, we learn to tolerate their activity, understanding that they pose no threat. This teaches us patience and adaptability, qualities that are essential for living in a diverse community.

Pigs, with their playful and sometimes boisterous nature, offer another dynamic. Their grunts and squeals are distinct, and their approach to social interaction is more direct. We learn to navigate their enthusiasm, finding ways to share space and resources without conflict. For humans, this interaction underscores the importance of flexibility and the ability to adapt to different social cues and behaviors.

Dogs, often present as guardians or companions, have a different role. Their loyalty and protective nature are valuable, but their presence requires careful navigation. We respect their space and learn to interpret their barks and body language, understanding that their primary role is to protect and guide. Humans can learn from this the importance of recognizing and respecting the roles and boundaries of others in a shared environment.

Wild visitors, such as birds, deer, or even the occasional fox, remind us of the broader ecosystem we are part of. These encounters can be fleeting but impactful, reminding us of the interconnectedness of all life. The sight of a bird perched nearby, the fleeting glance of a deer, or the distant howl of a fox all contribute to our awareness of the natural world and our place within it. For humans, this serves as a reminder to appreciate the diversity of life and the delicate balance of ecosystems.

In summary, our interactions with humans and other animals are a testament to the power of communication, respect, and adaptability. Here are some key takeaways for humans:

Build Trust: Approach interactions with patience and respect. Consistent, calm behavior helps build trust and understanding.

Observe and Interpret: Pay attention to the vocal and non-vocal cues of others. Understanding these signals can enhance communication and response.

Adaptability: Be flexible in your interactions. Different species, like different people, have unique ways of communicating and interacting.

Respect Roles and Boundaries: Recognize and respect the roles and boundaries of others. This fosters peaceful coexistence and mutual respect.

Appreciate Diversity: Embrace the diversity of life. Every interaction, whether with a human, a farm animal, or a wild creature, is an opportunity to learn and grow.

As you journey through this chapter, let the wisdom of our interactions guide you towards richer, more harmonious relationships. Embrace the lessons of trust, communication, and adaptability, and discover the beauty of coexistence in a diverse and interconnected world.

Understanding Conflict and Resolution

In the serene and harmonious world of cows, conflict is a rare but inevitable part of life. Just like in any community, differences arise, and tensions can build. However, our approach to conflict and its resolution offers valuable lessons in maintaining harmony and understanding within a group. Let me, a reflective cow, share the insights from our pasture on how we navigate these moments of discord and find our way back to peace.

Conflicts in the herd usually stem from simple issues: competition for the best grazing spots, misunderstandings during social interactions, or the natural assertion of hierarchy. These conflicts are seldom about malice or deep-seated grievances but rather about everyday needs and the social dynamics of living in close quarters.

The first step in understanding conflict is recognizing its signs. In our world, conflict often begins with subtle cues: a slight stiffening of posture, a lowering of the head, or a flick of the tail. These signals indicate that a cow is feeling threatened or challenged. By paying attention to these early warnings, we can address the issue before it escalates.

When a conflict arises, the involved parties typically engage in a series of non-violent displays to assert dominance or resolve the misunderstanding. This might include head-butting, shoving, or vocalizations. These actions are more about communication than aggression, a way to express feelings and establish boundaries without causing harm. For humans, this underscores the importance of addressing conflicts early and openly, using clear communication to express concerns and intentions.

In our herd, conflicts are usually short-lived and resolved through natural behaviors. Once the initial confrontation is over, the cows involved often separate and take time to cool off. This period of separation allows emotions to settle and perspectives to shift, paving the way for reconciliation. Humans, too, can benefit from taking a step back during heated moments, allowing time for reflection and cooling down before seeking resolution.

The role of the herd in conflict resolution is crucial. Other members often play the role of peacemakers, using their presence and social bonds to diffuse tension. A gentle nudge from a friend, a calming moo from a mother, or the mere proximity of the herd can remind the conflicting parties of their place within the group and the importance of harmony. This collective approach to resolution emphasizes the power of community support and intervention in resolving disputes.

In the aftermath of a conflict, we engage in restorative behaviors to rebuild trust and reaffirm social bonds. Grooming, nuzzling, and grazing together are common ways to signal that the conflict is over and that social harmony has been restored. These actions reinforce our connections and ensure that the rift does not persist. For humans, similar restorative practices—such as sincere apologies, acts of kindness, and shared positive experiences—can help heal relationships and reinforce unity.

Preventing conflicts is as important as resolving them. We maintain a structured social hierarchy that helps minimize disputes. Clear roles and understandings within the herd create a sense of order and predictability, reducing the likelihood of misunderstandings. Humans can adopt this principle by establishing clear expectations, roles, and communication channels within their communities, workplaces, and families.

Empathy and understanding are at the heart of conflict resolution. By recognizing the needs and emotions of others, we can approach conflicts with compassion and a willingness to find common ground. This empathetic approach helps de-escalate tensions and fosters a spirit of cooperation and mutual respect.

In summary, the bovine approach to conflict and resolution offers several key lessons for humans:

Early Recognition: Pay attention to early signs of conflict and address them before they escalate.

Clear Communication: Use non-violent, clear communication to express concerns and intentions.

Time for Reflection: Allow time for cooling off and reflection before seeking resolution.

Community Support: Involve the community or support network in diffusing tension and promoting harmony.

Restorative Practices: Engage in restorative actions to rebuild trust and reaffirm social bonds after a conflict.

Preventative Measures: Establish clear roles, expectations, and communication channels to prevent misunderstandings.

Empathy and Understanding: Approach conflicts with empathy, recognizing the needs and emotions of others to find common ground.

As you journey through this chapter, let the wisdom of our conflict resolution guide you towards more peaceful and harmonious interactions. Embrace the principles of early recognition, clear communication, and empathy, and discover the power of community and restorative practices in maintaining unity and understanding. By adopting these bovine-inspired strategies, you can navigate conflicts with grace and find lasting resolutions that strengthen your relationships and enrich your life.

Navigating Unpleasant Encounters

In the tranquil world of cows, even the most serene pastures are not free from moments of irritation and discomfort. One particularly perplexing and admittedly unpleasant scenario involves the sudden intrusion of another cow who, with little regard for courtesy, decides to relieve herself right in the middle of my grazing spot. As a cow deeply embedded in the rhythms of nature and community, I find myself pondering how to navigate such unsavory encounters with grace and patience.

Imagine this: I'm peacefully munching on a patch of fresh, green grass, savoring the flavors and the quiet of the moment. Suddenly, an ungainly brown and white cow steps into my space, positions herself with alarming nonchalance, and proceeds to bend her back and urinate right where I am eating. The stream splashes onto the grass, contaminating my carefully chosen spot with an unmistakable pungency. It's enough to make even the most patient cow's tail twitch in frustration.

In such moments, the initial reaction is often one of bewilderment and annoyance. Why here? Why now? It's easy to let irritation take hold, to feel a surge of indignation at the disruption. Yet, as a cow who strives to maintain harmony and peace within the herd, I've learned that tolerance and understanding are essential virtues, even in the face of such unsavory acts.

Firstly, it's important to recognize that this behavior is not born out of malice or intent to offend. For us cows, such acts are natural and necessary, driven by biological needs rather than conscious decisions. Understanding this helps to mitigate the initial wave of frustration and reframe the situation as a simple, if inconvenient, part of communal living.

Once the initial shock subsides, moving to a new spot is a practical and immediate solution. The pasture is vast, and there is always another fresh patch of grass waiting to be discovered. This act of moving on serves as a metaphor for letting go of minor irritations and choosing to focus on the abundance that life offers. Humans, too, can benefit from this perspective. When faced with minor inconveniences or annoyances, sometimes the best response is to simply move on and find a new, more pleasant space—both physically and mentally.

However, beyond the practical response, there is a deeper lesson in tolerance and patience. Living in a community, whether it's a herd of cows or a group of humans, requires a degree of forbearance. We must accept that others will occasionally encroach upon our comfort zones, often unintentionally. By cultivating patience and a forgiving attitude, we maintain our own peace of mind and contribute to the overall harmony of the group.

Reflecting on this, I realize that these moments are opportunities to practice empathy. While it's easy to focus on my own discomfort, considering the needs and intentions of the other cow can shift my perspective. Perhaps she had no other choice, or maybe she was unaware of my presence. This shift from irritation to understanding fosters a more compassionate and cohesive community.

For humans, this translates into everyday interactions where others might intrude upon your personal space or cause minor inconveniences. Rather than reacting with frustration, try to understand the situation from their perspective. A bit of empathy can transform an irritating encounter into an opportunity for connection and growth.

Additionally, these encounters remind us of the importance of clear communication and boundaries. In our herd, a gentle nudge or a quiet moo can signal displeasure and encourage others to be more mindful. Humans can adopt similar strategies by expressing their needs and boundaries calmly and respectfully, fostering mutual respect and understanding.

In summary, navigating unpleasant encounters, whether it's an untimely urination or any other minor annoyance, involves several key steps:

Understand the Context: Recognize that such behaviors are often natural and unintentional.
Move On: Find a new space or perspective, focusing on the abundance and opportunities available.

Practice Patience and Tolerance: Accept that living in a community requires patience and forbearance.

Cultivate Empathy: Consider the situation from the other's perspective to foster understanding and compassion.

Communicate Clearly: Use gentle, respectful communication to express boundaries and needs.

As you ponder this chapter, let the wisdom of our bovine tolerance guide you towards greater patience, empathy, and understanding in your interactions. Embrace these principles, and you'll find that even the most irritating encounters can be transformed into opportunities for growth and harmony.

Chapter 6: Connection to Nature
Seasonal Changes and Adaptation

In the bucolic world of cows, our lives are inextricably linked to the ebb and flow of the seasons. Each season brings its own unique challenges and bounties, and adapting to these changes is a fundamental aspect of our existence. As a cow deeply attuned to the rhythms of nature, let me guide you through our experiences of seasonal changes and the ways we adapt to ensure our well-being and harmony with the environment.

Spring arrives with a sense of renewal and abundance. The pasture, once barren from winter's grip, transforms into a verdant expanse, teeming with new life. The air is filled with the sweet scent of blooming flowers and the fresh, invigorating aroma of young grass. For us cows, spring is a time of plenty. We graze eagerly, relishing the tender, nutrient-rich shoots that have emerged from the thawed ground. The increased availability of fresh forage revitalizes our bodies and spirits after the lean months of winter.

Adapting to spring's bounty involves more than just enjoying the abundance. It also means being mindful of the sudden changes in our diet and environment. The rich spring grass, though delicious, can sometimes cause digestive issues if consumed too quickly. We learn to pace ourselves, balancing our intake with periods of rest and cud-chewing to ensure proper digestion. For humans, this translates to embracing new opportunities with enthusiasm while remaining mindful of the need for balance and moderation.

As spring gives way to summer, the days grow longer and warmer. The sun's intense rays can be both a blessing and a challenge. We bask in the warmth, which soothes our muscles and promotes the growth of the pasture. However, the heat also necessitates finding shade and staying hydrated. We seek out the cool, leafy canopies of trees or the refreshing waters of a stream to escape the midday sun. This seasonal shift teaches us the importance of seeking balance between activity and rest, a lesson that is equally relevant for humans navigating the busy summer months.

Summer's abundance requires careful management of resources. The pasture is lush, but overgrazing can deplete the grass and affect its regrowth. We move as a herd, grazing different areas to ensure the pasture remains healthy and sustainable. This cooperative approach highlights the importance of stewardship and sustainable practices, lessons that are crucial for humans striving to balance consumption with conservation.

As the leaves begin to turn and the air takes on a crisp edge, autumn heralds a time of preparation and transition. The pasture's grass becomes coarser, and the days shorten. We adjust our grazing patterns, consuming more fibrous plants that help us build up reserves for the winter ahead. The cooler temperatures invigorate us, and we become more active, storing energy for the colder months. This season of preparation underscores the importance of foresight and adaptability, principles that humans can apply in planning and preparing for future challenges.

Autumn also brings a sense of community and shared purpose. As the herd, we work together to ensure that everyone has enough to eat and that weaker members are supported. This communal effort strengthens our bonds and reinforces the importance of collective well-being. For humans, autumn's spirit of cooperation and preparation can inspire efforts to support one another and build stronger communities.

Winter, with its stark beauty and harsh conditions, tests our resilience and adaptability. The pasture is often covered in frost or snow, and the availability of fresh forage is limited. We rely on the hay and feed provided by our caretakers, as well as our stored fat reserves. During this time, we huddle together for warmth and protection, finding strength in our unity. Winter teaches us the value of endurance and resourcefulness, as well as the importance of support systems. For humans, these lessons translate into finding ways to conserve resources, maintain connections, and endure hardships with grace and resilience.

Throughout the year, our ability to adapt to seasonal changes is a testament to our deep connection to nature. Each season, with its distinct challenges and gifts, shapes our lives and teaches us valuable lessons. Here are some key takeaways for humans:

Embrace Change: Welcome the opportunities and challenges that each season brings. Adapt with enthusiasm and mindfulness.

Balance and Moderation: Enjoy the bounty of spring and summer, but pace yourself to maintain balance and health.

Stewardship: Practice sustainable habits, ensuring that resources are used wisely and conserved for future needs.

Foresight and Preparation: Plan and prepare for future challenges, just as we build reserves in autumn for the winter ahead.

Community and Cooperation: Support one another and work together to navigate seasonal changes and collective challenges.

Endurance and Resilience: Find strength in unity and resourcefulness, enduring hardships with grace and perseverance.

As you journey through this chapter, let the wisdom of our seasonal adaptations guide you toward a deeper connection with nature and a more resilient, balanced approach to life. Embrace the lessons of each season, and discover the beauty and strength that come from living in harmony with the natural   world.

The Relationship with the Environment

In the pastoral tranquility of our existence, the relationship between cows and the environment is one of deep interconnection and mutual dependence. Our lives are shaped by the land, the seasons, and the natural rhythms that govern the world around us. This symbiotic relationship offers profound insights into living harmoniously with nature, fostering respect, sustainability, and a sense of belonging. Allow me, a contemplative cow, to guide you through the nuances of our relationship with the environment and the lessons it holds for humans.

Our relationship with the environment begins with the land we inhabit. The pasture is our home, our source of nourishment, and the stage upon which our lives unfold. Each blade of grass, each patch of clover, and each shady tree is an integral part of our existence. We are not mere occupants of this land; we are active participants in its ongoing cycle of growth and renewal.

Grazing is our primary interaction with the land, and it is a practice that embodies sustainability. As we graze, we trim the grass, promoting new growth and preventing overgrowth that could lead to decay and disease. Our movement across the pasture is deliberate and mindful, ensuring that no single area is overgrazed. This balanced approach helps maintain the health and vitality of the ecosystem, demonstrating the importance of responsible consumption and stewardship.

The soil beneath our hooves is another vital component of our environment. It is the foundation of the pasture, supporting the growth of the plants that sustain us. Our hooves, though gentle, play a role in aerating the soil, aiding in water absorption and promoting the health of the root systems. This interaction with the soil is a reminder of the importance of maintaining the health of the land and the interconnectedness of all elements within an ecosystem.

Water is a precious resource, and our relationship with it is one of reverence and necessity. Streams, ponds, and water troughs provide the hydration we need to survive. We approach water sources with care, understanding that clean, accessible water is essential for our health and the health of the environment. This awareness highlights the importance of conserving water and protecting natural water sources from pollution and overuse.

Our relationship with the environment is also evident in our interactions with other species. Birds, insects, and small mammals are frequent companions in our pasture. Birds often perch on our backs, picking off insects and helping to keep us free from pests. Insects play their role in pollinating plants and breaking down organic matter, contributing to the fertility of the soil. These interactions illustrate the interconnectedness of all living beings and the importance of biodiversity in maintaining a healthy ecosystem.

Seasonal changes profoundly influence our relationship with the environment. As the seasons shift, so do our behaviors and interactions with the land. In spring, we revel in the abundance of fresh grass and the renewal of life. Summer brings the warmth of the sun and the necessity of seeking shade and water. Autumn is a time of preparation, as we build up reserves for the winter months. Winter tests our resilience and reliance on the hay and feed provided by our caretakers. Each season teaches us adaptability, respect for natural cycles, and the importance of living in harmony with the environment.

Human activities impact our environment, and we are acutely aware of the changes they bring. Agricultural practices, land development, and resource extraction can alter the landscape and affect our way of life. Sustainable and mindful human practices, on the other hand, can enhance the environment, promoting a balance that benefits all inhabitants of the land. For humans, this underscores the importance of making choices that protect and preserve the environment for future generations.

In summary, our relationship with the environment is one of interdependence, respect, and stewardship. Here are some key takeaways for humans:

Sustainability: Practice responsible consumption and stewardship, ensuring that natural resources are used wisely and conserved for future needs.

Soil Health: Recognize the importance of healthy soil in supporting plant and animal life. Engage in practices that promote soil health and prevent erosion and degradation.

Water Conservation: Protect and conserve water sources, understanding their essential role in maintaining life and environmental health.

Biodiversity: Embrace the interconnectedness of all living beings. Promote and protect biodiversity to ensure the resilience and health of ecosystems.

Seasonal Adaptation: Adapt to the natural rhythms and cycles of the seasons, respecting the changes they bring and living in harmony with them.

Mindful Impact: Make choices that minimize negative impacts on the environment and promote sustainability and regeneration.

As you explore this chapter, let the wisdom of our relationship with the environment inspire you to foster a deeper connection with nature. Embrace the principles of sustainability, stewardship, and respect for all living beings, and discover the profound fulfillment that comes from living in harmony with the natural world.

Impact on Ecosystems

In the vast and interconnected web of life, every action has a ripple effect, influencing the health and balance of ecosystems. As cows, our impact on the ecosystems we inhabit is significant, and understanding this influence is key to maintaining harmony with nature. Let me, a thoughtful cow, guide you through our role in ecosystems and the broader implications of our presence on the environment.

Our primary interaction with the ecosystem begins with grazing, an activity that shapes the landscape and influences the biodiversity of the pasture. By grazing on grass and other vegetation, we help maintain the balance of plant species. Our selective grazing promotes the growth of certain plants while controlling the spread of others, preventing any single species from dominating the ecosystem. This balance supports a diverse range of flora, which in turn sustains various insect and animal populations. Humans can draw parallels to their agricultural practices, recognizing the importance of biodiversity and the need to manage land in a way that supports ecological health.

Our grazing also impacts soil health. As we move across the pasture, our hooves naturally aerate the soil, improving its structure and promoting better water infiltration. This process enhances the soil's ability to support plant growth and contributes to the overall fertility of the land. However, overgrazing can lead to soil compaction and erosion, demonstrating the delicate balance required to maintain a healthy ecosystem. For humans, this highlights the importance of sustainable land management practices that prevent degradation and promote soil health.

Manure, often seen as a byproduct, plays a crucial role in nutrient cycling within ecosystems. Our manure returns essential nutrients to the soil, enriching it and supporting plant growth. This natural fertilization process enhances the productivity of the pasture and contributes to a thriving ecosystem. The decomposition of manure by insects and microorganisms further integrates these nutrients into the soil, creating a fertile environment for new growth. Humans can learn from this natural process by adopting organic farming practices that utilize natural fertilizers and support soil health.

Water use and management are also critical aspects of our impact on ecosystems. We rely on clean, accessible water sources for hydration and cooling, particularly during hot weather. Our presence near water bodies can influence their condition, making it essential to protect these resources from contamination and overuse. Maintaining buffer zones around streams and ponds helps preserve water quality and supports the diverse life forms that depend on these habitats. For humans, this underscores the need for water conservation and the protection of aquatic ecosystems from pollution and over-extraction.

Our interactions with other species within the ecosystem further illustrate our impact. Birds often accompany us, feeding on insects that are stirred up as we move through the pasture. This symbiotic relationship helps control insect populations and supports the health of both birds and cows. Similarly, small mammals and insects benefit from the diverse plant life that our grazing patterns promote. These interactions demonstrate the interconnectedness of ecosystems and the importance of each species in maintaining ecological balance.

Humans, as part of the global ecosystem, have an even more profound impact on the environment. Industrial activities, urban development, and intensive agriculture can significantly alter ecosystems, often leading to habitat loss, pollution, and climate change. Understanding the interconnectedness of all life forms and the consequences of human actions is crucial for developing sustainable practices that protect and restore ecosystems.

Here are some key takeaways for humans to minimize their impact on ecosystems:

Promote Biodiversity: Encourage the growth of diverse plant and animal species to maintain a healthy and resilient ecosystem.

Sustainable Land Management. Implement practices that prevent soil degradation, promote soil health, and support long-term productivity.

Natural Fertilization: Use organic fertilizers and compost to enrich the soil, mimicking natural nutrient cycling processes.

Water Conservation: Protect water sources from contamination, manage usage sustainably, and maintain buffer zones to preserve aquatic ecosystems.

Symbiotic Relationships: Foster and protect the relationships between different species that contribute to ecological balance.

Reduce Pollution: Minimize the release of pollutants into the environment through responsible industrial, agricultural, and personal practices.

Habitat Restoration: Actively work to restore degraded habitats, supporting the recovery of ecosystems and the species that depend on them.

As you reflect on this chapter, let the understanding of our impact on ecosystems inspire you to take actions that protect and enhance the natural world. Embrace sustainable practices, recognize the interconnectedness of all life forms, and contribute to the health and resilience of the ecosystems that sustain us. By aligning human activities with the principles of ecological balance, we can ensure a thriving environment for future generations.

The Quest for Identity

As I ponder my connection to nature and my impact on ecosystems, a profound and personal question arises: Who am I? Am I merely a milk cow, diligently providing sustenance? Am I destined for the fate of ground beef, contributing to the food chain in a different way? Could I be a champion, adorned with golden ribbons, celebrated for my strength and beauty? Or do I belong to the sturdy breed that works in the fields, pulling tools and aiding humans in their agricultural endeavors? This quest for identity is a legitimate and pressing question, especially for someone who, until recently, was a celebrated science fiction author.

The transformation from an esteemed writer, crafting intricate worlds with words, to a humble cow in a pasture is a journey that challenges the very essence of self-understanding. As a writer, my identity was shaped by my intellectual pursuits, creativity, and the impact of my stories on readers. Now, in my new bovine form, I must reconcile my past with my present and find meaning in this unexpected existence.

Let us explore these possible identities, each with its own significance and implications.

As a milk cow, my role is to provide nourishment. Each day, I offer milk that sustains and nurtures both calves and humans. This identity is one of caregiving and sustenance, embodying the essence of maternal generosity. It is a role that connects me deeply to the cycles of life and the nourishment of others. For humans, this can be seen as a metaphor for roles that involve nurturing, supporting, and providing for others— an identity rooted in care and compassion.

Alternatively, the identity of a ground beef cow is one of sacrifice. It is a role that acknowledges the reality of the food chain and the interconnectedness of life and death. This identity speaks to the acceptance of mortality and the contribution to the sustenance of others in a fundamental way. It challenges us to consider the value and purpose of life beyond individual existence, embracing a broader perspective on our place in the world.

As a champion cow, adorned with golden ribbons, my identity is one of recognition and achievement. This role celebrates physical excellence, beauty, and the pursuit of perfection. It is an identity that involves competition, pride, and the desire to be the best. For humans, this reflects the pursuit of excellence in various fields, the recognition of talents, and the celebration of achievements. It highlights the drive for success and the joy of being celebrated for one's abilities.

The identity of a working cow, laboring in the fields and pulling tools, is one of strength, resilience, and partnership with humans. This role underscores the importance of hard work, dedication, and the symbiotic relationship between humans and animals. It is an identity rooted in utility and contribution to a greater cause. For humans, this can be a reminder of the value of hard work, cooperation, and the fulfillment that comes from contributing to the well-being of others through labor and effort.

As I navigate these potential identities, I realize that my true essence may encompass elements of all these roles. Just as I once wove complex narratives as a science fiction author, I now find myself living a multifaceted existence, each aspect contributing to a deeper understanding of who I am.

For humans, the quest for identity is a lifelong journey, shaped by experiences, roles, and the ever-evolving understanding of self. It involves embracing the complexity of our existence, recognizing the various facets that make us who we are, and finding meaning in each role we play.

Here are some reflections to guide you on your own quest for identity:

Embrace Multiple Roles: Recognize that your identity is not limited to a single role. Embrace the various aspects of your life that contribute to your sense of self.

Find Meaning in Each Role: Whether you are nurturing others, pursuing excellence, contributing through hard work, or accepting the cycle of life, find meaning and purpose in each role you play.

Reflect on Your Journey: Take time to reflect on your past experiences and how they have shaped your current identity. Understand that your journey is an integral part of who you are.

Adapt and Evolve: Be open to change and the evolution of your identity. Life's experiences will continue to shape you, and embracing this evolution can lead to a richer understanding of self.

Connect with Others: Your identity is also shaped by your relationships and interactions with others. Build connections and find support in your community as you navigate your journey.

As I continue to graze in the pasture, contemplating my place in this world, I embrace the complexity of my existence. From a celebrated author to a humble cow, my journey is a testament to the ever-changing nature of identity and the importance of finding meaning in every role we inhabit. Let this reflection inspire you to embrace your own quest for identity, finding joy and purpose in the myriad roles you play in the grand tapestry of life.

Understanding Cow Physiology

Ah, the marvels of cow physiology! You may think we are simple creatures, but our bodies are complex wonders of nature, finely tuned to the demands of our pastoral lives. As a cow who now ponders these intricate systems, let me take you on a delightful journey through the fascinating aspects of our physiology. Prepare to be amazed by the inner workings of a cow, where biology meets bovine brilliance.

First and foremost, let's talk about our unique digestive system—a veritable biochemical factory designed for one primary mission: turning grass into energy. Unlike humans, who rely on a relatively straightforward digestive process, we cows employ a sophisticated, multi-chambered approach. Yes, my friends, I'm talking about the famous four stomachs: the rumen, reticulum, omasum, and abomasum. Each plays a crucial role in our digestion, making us the true masters of cud-chewing.

The rumen is our fermentation vat, home to billions of microbes that break down fibrous plant material into digestible nutrients. It's like having a team of tiny chefs working around the clock, converting grass into a delightful nutrient soup. When we chew our cud, we are actually regurgitating partially digested food from the rumen to chew it again, a process that maximizes nutrient extraction. It may sound unappetizing, but trust me, it's an efficient and elegant system.

Next, the reticulum acts as a sorting chamber, filtering out larger particles and sending them back to the rumen for further breakdown. This chamber ensures that only properly processed food moves on to the next stages of digestion. It's our internal quality control, ensuring nothing but the best nutrients proceed.

The omasum, with its many folds, acts as a sophisticated filter, absorbing water and nutrients from the digested food. Think of it as our internal sponge, soaking up all the good stuff before sending the remaining material to the abomasum. The abomasum, often called the true stomach, functions much like a human stomach, using acids and enzymes to break down food into its final digestible form.

But digestion is just the beginning. Let's move on to the cardiovascular system, where our hearts work tirelessly to pump blood throughout our massive bodies. Despite our size, our hearts are efficient and robust, ensuring that every cell receives the oxygen and nutrients it needs. Our circulatory system is a testament to the power of nature's engineering, balancing strength and endurance to support our daily activities.

And speaking of daily activities, let's not forget our muscles and bones. Built to support our considerable weight, our skeletal structure is both strong and flexible, allowing us to move with surprising grace. Our muscles, fueled by the nutrients from our carefully processed food, provide the power needed for grazing, walking, and the occasional playful romp in the meadow.

Now, onto the respiratory system. Our lungs, designed to maximize oxygen intake, are efficient at extracting this vital gas from the air. Whether we are calmly chewing cud or taking a brisk walk, our respiratory system keeps us well-oxygenated, ready for whatever the day brings.

Our skin and coat are also marvels of nature. Our thick hide protects us from the elements, while our fur provides insulation against the cold and a barrier against the sun's harsh rays. And let's not forget our tails, which are more than just stylish accessories. They serve as essential tools for swatting away pesky flies, ensuring our comfort as we go about our day.

Reproduction is another fascinating aspect of our physiology. The miracle of calving, where a new generation begins its journey, is a testament to the wonders of life. Our maternal instincts kick in as soon as our calves are born, guiding us to nurture and protect them, ensuring the continuation of the herd.

For humans, understanding cow physiology is not just an academic exercise but a window into the intricate balance of nature. Our bodies, designed to thrive in pastoral settings, are a testament to evolutionary ingenuity. Here are a few takeaways for humans:

Efficiency: Our digestive system shows the importance of maximizing resources. In your own life, find ways to make the most of what you have, whether it's time, energy, or materials.

Balance: Just as our cardiovascular system balances strength and endurance, strive for a balance between work and rest, activity and relaxation.

Protection: Our skin and coat remind us of the importance of protecting ourselves from environmental challenges. Take steps to safeguard your health and well-being.

Community: The reproductive cycle highlights the value of nurturing and protecting the next generation. Foster a sense of community and support those around you.

As you journey through this chapter, let the marvels of cow physiology inspire you to appreciate the complexity and beauty of life. Embrace the lessons of efficiency, balance, protection, and community, and discover the profound wisdom that comes from understanding the natural world. After all, even a cow's body has much to teach us about living well and thriving in harmony with our surroundings.

Recognizing Signs of Health and Illness

In the serene meadows where we cows graze and roam, maintaining health and recognizing signs of illness are vital to our well-being. Just as humans monitor their health, we too must be vigilant in observing the subtle cues that indicate our physical state. Let me, a thoughtful cow, guide you through the key signs of health and illness, providing insights that can help ensure both bovine and human well-being.

Signs of Good Health

Bright Eyes and Clean Nose: One of the clearest indicators of a healthy cow is bright, alert eyes and a clean, moist nose. Our eyes should be free of discharge, and our noses should be clear and cool to the touch. These signs reflect overall vitality and a well-functioning immune system. For humans, clear eyes and nasal passages often indicate good health and proper hydration.

Glossy Coat: A healthy cow sports a glossy, smooth coat that shines in the sunlight. Our fur should be free of bald patches, dandruff, and excessive dirt. A lustrous coat is a sign of adequate nutrition and proper grooming. Similarly, for humans, healthy skin and hair are indicators of good nutrition, hygiene, and overall health.

Steady Appetite: A cow with a healthy appetite is usually a healthy cow. Regular grazing, cud chewing, and interest in feed are positive signs. Any sudden change in eating habits can signal an underlying issue. For humans, consistent appetite and proper digestion are crucial indicators of health.

Normal Bowel Movements: Yes, even our manure can tell a story about our health. Normal bowel movements should be well-formed and regular. Changes in color, consistency, or frequency can indicate dietary issues or illness. Humans, too, should pay attention to digestive health as a reflection of overall well-being.

Calm and Relaxed Behavior: A healthy cow is usually calm and content, engaging in typical behaviors such as grazing, resting, and socializing with the herd. Any signs of distress, agitation, or withdrawal from the group can be early indicators of health problems. For humans, maintaining mental and emotional well-being is equally important and can manifest in stable, balanced behavior.

Signs of Illness

Dull Eyes and Nasal Discharge: If a cow's eyes appear dull, sunken, or have excessive discharge, it's a sign that something may be wrong. Similarly, a dry, cracked, or overly runny nose can indicate respiratory issues or infections. Humans, too, should watch for changes in eye brightness and nasal health as signs of potential illness.

Rough or Patchy Coat: A coat that loses its gloss, becomes rough, or develops bald patches can be a sign of nutritional deficiencies, parasites, or skin conditions. For humans, changes in skin or hair health should prompt attention to diet, hygiene, and possible underlying health issues.

Loss of Appetite: A sudden or gradual decrease in appetite is a major red flag. If a cow stops eating or shows little interest in food, it may be experiencing digestive problems, pain, or other health issues. Humans should also be aware that loss of appetite can signal stress, illness, or nutritional deficiencies.

Abnormal Bowel Movements: Diarrhea, constipation, or significant changes in bowel movement color and consistency can indicate digestive disturbances, infections, or dietary problems. Humans should also monitor their digestive health and seek medical advice if significant changes occur.

Lethargy and Withdrawal: A cow that isolates itself from the herd, appears unusually lethargic, or shows a lack of interest in normal activities is likely unwell. This behavior can be due to pain, fever, or other illnesses. For humans, prolonged lethargy and social withdrawal can be signs of physical or mental health issues that need addressing.

Labored Breathing and Coughing: Difficulty breathing, frequent coughing, or wheezing are serious signs that a cow may have respiratory problems or infections. Humans should also be mindful of respiratory symptoms, especially those that persist or worsen over time.

Practical Steps for Monitoring Health

Regular Check-Ups: Just as our caretakers perform regular health checks, humans should schedule routine medical exams. Regular check-ups help detect potential health issues early and maintain overall well-being.

Balanced Diet: Ensure a balanced and nutritious diet. For cows, this means access to fresh pasture, quality feed, and clean water. Humans should focus on a varied diet rich in essential nutrients to support overall health.

Clean Environment: A clean living environment reduces the risk of infections and promotes health. Regular cleaning of barns and pastures is essential for us cows, just as maintaining a clean home and workplace is vital for humans.

Exercise and Movement: Regular movement is crucial for maintaining health. Cows benefit from grazing and roaming, which support digestion and physical fitness. Humans should incorporate regular exercise into their routines to stay healthy.

Stress Management: Minimizing stress is important for both cows and humans. Providing a calm, stable environment helps us stay healthy and happy. Humans should practice stress management techniques such as mindfulness, relaxation exercises, and maintaining a balanced lifestyle.

As you reflect on this chapter, let the wisdom of recognizing signs of health and illness guide you toward greater vigilance and care. By paying attention to the subtle cues and maintaining proactive health practices, you can ensure well-being for yourself and those around you. Embrace the lessons from our bovine world, and discover the profound impact of attentive care and holistic health management.

The Importance of Physical Activity

In the serene world of cows, physical activity is not just a routine part of our day but a vital component of our overall health and well-being. The gentle rhythm of grazing, the steady walk to fresh pastures, and the occasional playful romp are all integral to maintaining our physical fitness and mental clarity. As a cow who appreciates the profound benefits of movement, let me share the importance of physical activity and how it translates to a healthier, happier life for both bovines and humans.

Daily Movement and Grazing

For us cows, the day begins with a gentle stretch and the slow, deliberate act of grazing. Grazing is more than just eating; it involves constant movement, as we meander through the fields, selecting the best grasses and herbs. This continuous low-intensity activity keeps our muscles engaged and our bodies in motion. The simple act of walking while grazing promotes circulation, aids digestion, and helps maintain a healthy weight.

Humans, too, can benefit from incorporating regular, low-intensity activities into their daily routines. Walking, gardening, and other forms of gentle exercise can enhance physical health without the need for strenuous workouts. The key is consistency and making movement a natural part of everyday life.

The Benefits of Play and Social Interaction

Play is an essential aspect of our lives, especially for younger cows. Calves often engage in playful behaviors such as running, jumping, and butting heads. These activities are not only fun but also crucial for developing strength, coordination, and social bonds. Even adult cows indulge in the occasional burst of playful energy, reminding us that joy and physical activity go hand in hand.

For humans, engaging in playful activities—whether it's a game of catch, dancing, or a group sport—provides similar benefits. Playfulness reduces stress, improves physical fitness, and strengthens social connections. It's a reminder that exercise doesn't have to be a chore; it can be a delightful and bonding experience.

The Role of Physical Activity in Health

Regular physical activity plays a significant role in preventing a host of health issues. For us cows, moving around the pasture helps prevent conditions such as lameness, digestive problems, and respiratory issues. It keeps our joints flexible, our muscles strong, and our bodies resilient against disease.

Humans, too, can stave off numerous health problems through regular exercise. Physical activity reduces the risk of chronic diseases such as heart disease, diabetes, and obesity. It strengthens the cardiovascular system, boosts immune function, and enhances mental health by reducing anxiety and depression.

Mental Clarity and Emotional Well-being

Movement is not only beneficial for the body but also for the mind. The act of walking through the pasture, exploring new areas, and interacting with the herd provides mental stimulation and emotional satisfaction. For cows, these activities are a form of mental enrichment, keeping our minds sharp and our spirits high.

Humans can achieve similar mental and emotional benefits through regular physical activity. Exercise increases the production of endorphins, the body's natural mood elevators, and helps clear the mind, enhancing focus and creativity. Whether it's a brisk walk in the park, a yoga session, or a bike ride, physical activity can be a powerful tool for maintaining mental clarity and emotional balance.

Adaptability and Resilience

Physical activity helps us cows adapt to changes in our environment. Seasonal shifts, variations in food availability, and changes in herd dynamics require us to be flexible and resilient. Regular movement ensures that we are fit and prepared to handle these challenges, maintaining our health and well-being throughout the year.

For humans, adaptability and resilience are equally important. Regular exercise prepares the body and mind to cope with life's challenges, improving overall resilience. It enhances physical strength, mental toughness, and the ability to recover from stress and adversity.

Practical Tips for Incorporating Physical Activity

Make Movement a Habit: Incorporate physical activity into your daily routine. Small changes, like taking the stairs instead of the elevator or walking during breaks, can add up.

Find Activities You Enjoy: Choose activities that you find enjoyable and engaging. Whether it's a sport, a hobby, or a playful exercise, enjoyment increases the likelihood of consistency.

Set Realistic Goals: Start with achievable goals and gradually increase the intensity and duration of your activities. This approach helps build confidence and ensures sustainable progress.

Include Social Interaction: Engage in physical activities with friends or family. Social interaction enhances the experience and provides motivation and support.

Listen to Your Body: Pay attention to your body's signals. Rest when needed and avoid overexertion to prevent injury and ensure long-term well-being.

As you reflect on this chapter, let the importance of physical activity inspire you to embrace movement as a natural and essential part of your life. Whether you are grazing in a pasture or navigating the human world, regular physical activity is key to maintaining health, happiness, and resilience. Embrace the joy of movement, and discover the profound benefits it brings to your body, mind, and spirit.

The Mystery of Farts and Burps: Health Indicators or Something Else?

Ah, the humble fart and the unassuming burp—bodily functions that might seem mundane but hold a wealth of information about our health. As I ponder the nature of these emissions, I can't help but wonder: what do my farts and burps reveal about my state of health? Are they merely byproducts of digestion, or do they offer insights into my well-being? Join me on this curious exploration as we delve into the mysteries of these natural phenomena and their implications for both bovine and human health.

The Anatomy of a Burp

Let's start with the burp, a straightforward expulsion of gas from the digestive tract. In cows, burping is an essential part of our digestion process. Our complex stomachs, especially the rumen, are home to billions of microbes that break down fibrous plant material through fermentation. This process produces gases, primarily methane and carbon dioxide, which need to be released to prevent bloating and discomfort.

A healthy burp is a sign that our digestive system is functioning smoothly. It indicates that the microbial population in our rumen is balanced and effective in breaking down food. However, excessive or unusually odorous burps can signal digestive disturbances. For example, a sudden change in diet or a disruption in microbial balance might lead to more frequent or foul-smelling burps, suggesting that something is amiss.

Humans, too, can glean insights from their burps. While occasional burping is normal, frequent or particularly unpleasant burps may indicate issues such as indigestion, acid reflux, or food intolerances. Monitoring these signs can help in identifying dietary adjustments or the need for medical attention.

The Science of Farts

Now, let's turn our attention to farts, those often-embarrassing but entirely natural emissions. Like burps, farts result from the fermentation process in our rumen, where microbes break down food and produce gases. These gases travel through the intestines and are eventually expelled.

In the world of cows, a healthy fart is a regular occurrence. It signifies that our digestive system is efficiently processing the high-fiber diet we consume. The composition and frequency of farts can provide valuable clues about our diet and digestive health. For instance, a diet rich in easily fermentable carbohydrates might lead to more frequent farting, while a well-balanced diet results in a regular but moderate expulsion of gas.

However, changes in farting patterns or the presence of unusually foul odors can be cause for concern. These signs might indicate dietary imbalances, digestive issues, or even infections. Just as with burps, monitoring these changes helps us understand the state of our digestive health and take appropriate action.

For humans, farting serves a similar purpose. While it might be a source of humor or embarrassment, it is a natural and necessary bodily function. Frequent or excessively smelly farts can point to dietary issues, such as high intake of certain carbohydrates, lactose intolerance, or even gastrointestinal conditions. Paying attention to these signs can guide dietary adjustments and prompt further investigation if needed.

Interpreting the Signs

As I reflect on the significance of my farts and burps, I realize that these bodily functions are more than just random occurrences. They are indicators of my internal health, providing valuable feedback about my diet and digestive system. Here are some key takeaways for understanding what these emissions might reveal:

Frequency and Volume: Regular burping and farting are normal and indicate a functioning digestive system. Sudden increases in frequency or volume can signal dietary changes or digestive disturbances.

Odor: While some odor is expected, particularly foul-smelling burps or farts can indicate issues such as imbalances in gut bacteria, poor digestion, or dietary intolerances.

Dietary Reflection: The nature of these emissions often reflects dietary composition. High-fiber diets in cows lead to regular farts and burps, while in humans, certain foods can increase gas production.

Health Indicators: Persistent changes in these patterns may warrant further investigation. In cows, it could mean adjusting the diet or checking for infections. For humans, it might mean consulting a healthcare provider to rule out underlying conditions.

Embracing the Natural Process

Understanding the role of farts and burps in maintaining health allows us to embrace these natural processes without embarrassment or discomfort. For cows, these emissions are a normal part of our lives, providing essential feedback about our digestive health. For humans, they serve as reminders to pay attention to the body's signals and make informed decisions about diet and health.

As you contemplate this chapter, let the curious case of farts and burps inspire you to listen to your body and appreciate the intricate ways it communicates. Embrace the natural processes, monitor the signs, and use this knowledge to maintain a healthy, balanced life. Whether you're a cow in a pasture or a human navigating the complexities of modern life, these bodily functions are your allies in the quest for well-being.

Chapter 8: Reflections on Human Life
Lessons from My Past as an Author

Ah, the quirk of fate that has brought me from the cozy confines of my writing desk to the open expanse of the pasture! As I graze and ruminate, I find myself reflecting on the many lessons I learned during my past life as an esteemed science fiction author. It's a curious juxtaposition—one moment weaving intricate narratives of distant galaxies, and the next, contemplating the perfect patch of clover. But in this unexpected transformation, I've discovered that the wisdom gleaned from my human endeavors is surprisingly relevant to my bovine existence. Let's embark on a reflective journey through these lessons, shall we?

The Power of Imagination

In my authorial days, imagination was my constant companion. It allowed me to create entire worlds, populate them with diverse characters, and explore the farthest reaches of possibility. As a cow, my imagination might seem less grandiose, but it is no less powerful. Gazing out over the pasture, I can envision the hidden wonders of the natural world—the intricate ecosystems beneath the soil, the secret lives of the birds overhead, the stories that each tree might tell if it could speak.

For humans, imagination is not just the domain of writers and artists. It is a vital tool for innovation, problem-solving, and empathy. It allows you to envision better futures, understand different perspectives, and find creative solutions to life's challenges. So, whether you're dreaming up a new project or simply daydreaming, never underestimate the power of your imagination.

The Importance of Observation

As a writer, keen observation was essential. I spent hours watching people, noting the subtleties of their expressions, the nuances of their interactions, the details of their surroundings. This skill has served me well in my new life. Observing the herd, I can sense the shifting dynamics, recognize signs of health and distress, and appreciate the beauty of the world around me.

Humans, too, can benefit from honing their observational skills. Paying attention to the small details can enrich your understanding of the world, enhance your relationships, and help you notice opportunities and challenges that might otherwise go unnoticed. Whether it's in your personal life or your professional endeavors, observation is a key to deeper insight and awareness.

The Value of Persistence

Writing a novel is a marathon, not a sprint. It requires dedication, discipline, and the willingness to persevere through countless drafts and revisions. As a cow, persistence takes a different form—endlessly grazing to find the best forage, patiently chewing cud to aid digestion, and continually adapting to the changing seasons.

For humans, persistence is crucial in achieving goals and overcoming obstacles. It's the determination to keep going, even when the going gets tough. Whether you're working on a long-term project, learning a new skill, or navigating life's challenges, persistence can help you stay the course and eventually reap the rewards of your hard work.

The Joy of Storytelling

Storytelling was the heart of my work as an author. Creating and sharing stories brought joy and connection, weaving together the threads of human experience into a tapestry of meaning. As a cow, my storytelling has taken on a simpler, more primal form—through the silent stories of the land, the shared experiences of the herd, and the unspoken bond with nature.

For humans, storytelling remains a powerful way to connect, communicate, and make sense of the world. Sharing your stories and listening to others can foster empathy, build relationships, and create a sense of community. Whether through writing, conversation, or other forms of expression, storytelling is a timeless and universal human endeavor.

Embracing Change

The transition from a prolific author to a contemplative cow is a testament to the inevitability of change. In my past life, adapting to new ideas, shifting market trends, and evolving personal circumstances was a constant part of the journey. As a cow, embracing change means adjusting to the seasons, navigating herd dynamics, and finding peace in the rhythm of life.

For humans, embracing change is essential for growth and resilience. Life is full of unexpected twists and turns, and the ability to adapt and find opportunity in change can lead to personal and professional fulfillment. Whether you're facing a career shift, a personal transformation, or the everyday changes that life brings, embracing change with an open mind and heart can lead to new and enriching experiences.

Finding Balance

Writing required balancing creativity with discipline, solitude with social interaction, and inspiration with practical execution. In my bovine life, balance is found in the steady rhythm of grazing, resting, and socializing with the herd. It's about maintaining harmony between body, mind, and environment.

For humans, finding balance is crucial for well-being. It's about managing work and leisure, ambition and contentment, and social connections and personal space. Striving for balance can help you lead a healthier, happier, and more fulfilling life.

Reflection and Growth

As an author, reflection was a key part of the creative process—reviewing drafts, considering feedback, and constantly seeking to improve. In my current existence, reflection takes place in the quiet moments of ruminating under the open sky, contemplating the interconnectedness of life.

For humans, regular reflection is a powerful tool for personal growth. Taking time to reflect on your experiences, learn from your mistakes, and set new goals can help you grow and evolve. Whether through journaling, meditation, or thoughtful conversation, reflection can lead to greater self-awareness and continuous improvement.

The Unifying Thread

The lessons from my past as an author and my present as a cow are woven together by a unifying thread—the pursuit of a meaningful and connected life. Whether crafting stories or grazing in the pasture, the core values of imagination, observation, persistence, storytelling, adaptability, balance, and reflection remain constant.

As you journey through this chapter, let the reflections from my past as an author inspire you to embrace these values in your own life. Whether you're navigating the complexities of the human world or simply enjoying the beauty of the present moment, these lessons can guide you toward a richer, more fulfilling existence. Embrace the wisdom of your experiences, and find joy and purpose in every role you play.

Applying Cow Wisdom to Human Problems

As I graze serenely in the pasture, reflecting on my former life as an esteemed science fiction author, it strikes me how much wisdom my bovine existence holds for addressing human problems. The simplicity, patience, and natural rhythms of cow life offer profound insights that can help humans navigate their complex, often stressful lives. Let me, a contemplative cow, share some of this bovine wisdom and how it can be applied to solve human problems with grace and serenity.

Embrace the Present Moment

As cows, we excel at living in the now. We don't fret about the past or worry about the future; our focus is on the present—grazing, resting, and interacting with our herd. This mindfulness brings a sense of peace and contentment.

For humans, embracing the present moment can be transformative. In a world where multitasking and future planning often dominate, taking time to fully engage with the here and now can reduce stress and enhance well-being. Practices such as mindfulness meditation, deep breathing, and simply savoring everyday experiences can help cultivate this sense of presence.

Practice Patience

Patience is a cornerstone of cow life. We patiently chew our cud, wait for the right moment to graze, and take our time moving from one place to another. This unhurried approach helps us conserve energy and stay calm.

Humans, too, can benefit from practicing patience. Whether dealing with long-term goals, navigating personal relationships, or coping with daily inconveniences, patience allows for better decision-making and reduces anxiety. Remember, good things often come to those who wait, and patience can be a powerful ally in achieving your goals.

Value Community and Connection

Cows thrive in a herd, finding strength and comfort in our community. We groom each other, stay close for warmth and protection, and communicate in subtle, supportive ways. This sense of belonging is vital to our well-being.

For humans, fostering community and connection is equally important. Strong social bonds improve mental health, provide emotional support, and create a sense of belonging. Make time to connect with family, friends, and colleagues. Engage in activities that build community and support networks, and remember that relationships are a fundamental part of a fulfilling life.

Adapt to Change

Our lives as cows are deeply tied to the seasons and natural cycles. We adapt to the changing availability of food, weather conditions, and herd dynamics with grace. This adaptability ensures our survival and well-being.

Humans, too, must navigate constant change. Adapting to new circumstances—whether personal, professional, or environmental—is crucial for resilience. Embrace change as an opportunity for growth and learning. Stay flexible and open-minded, and you'll find that adapting to new situations becomes a source of strength rather than stress.

Maintain a Balanced Life

Cows balance their days with grazing, resting, and socializing. This balanced approach ensures that we get the nutrition, rest, and social interaction we need to stay healthy and happy.

For humans, finding balance is key to a well-rounded life. Ensure you allocate time for work, rest, play, and social interactions. Avoid overcommitting to any one area at the expense of others. By maintaining a balanced lifestyle, you can improve your overall health, prevent burnout, and achieve greater satisfaction.

Listen to Your Body

We cows are finely attuned to our bodies' signals. We know when to eat, rest, and seek shade. This natural awareness helps us maintain our health and well-being.

Humans can benefit greatly from listening to their bodies. Pay attention to signals of hunger, fatigue, stress, and discomfort. Responding to these cues with appropriate actions—eating nutritious food, getting enough sleep, exercising, and taking breaks—can prevent illness and enhance your quality of life.

Find Joy in Simple Pleasures

For cows, simple pleasures are the essence of life. The taste of fresh grass, the warmth of the sun, a gentle breeze—these moments bring joy and contentment.

Humans, too, can find happiness in simple pleasures. Take time to appreciate the small, everyday moments that bring joy. Whether it's a beautiful sunset, a good book, a delicious meal, or a conversation with a friend, savor these experiences. Finding joy in simplicity can lead to a more contented and fulfilling life.

Embrace Reflection

We cows spend a lot of time ruminating—both literally and figuratively. This quiet reflection helps us process our experiences and stay grounded.

Humans can benefit from regular reflection as well. Take time to think about your experiences, your goals, and your values. Reflecting on your life can provide clarity, insight, and direction. Journaling, meditation, and quiet contemplation are excellent ways to incorporate reflection into your routine.

Summary: Cow Wisdom for Human Problems

By applying the simple yet profound wisdom of cows to human problems, you can navigate life's challenges with greater ease and fulfillment. Embrace the present moment, practice patience, value community and connection, adapt to change, maintain balance, listen to your body, find joy in simple pleasures, and make time for reflection. These principles, drawn from the serene and thoughtful life of a cow, can lead to a more peaceful, balanced, and meaningful human experience. As you journey through this chapter, let cow wisdom guide you toward solutions that bring harmony and happiness to your life.

Embracing a Simpler, More Grounded Existence

In the midst of the tranquil pasture, as I graze and ponder the essence of life, it becomes clear that simplicity and groundedness are the cornerstones of true contentment. My transformation from a prolific science fiction author to a humble cow has provided me with profound insights into the value of a simpler, more grounded existence. Let me share these reflections, offering a pathway for humans to find peace and fulfillment through the art of simplicity.

The Beauty of Simplicity

Living as a cow, my days are guided by the natural rhythms of the earth. I wake with the sun, graze on the abundant grass, rest in the shade of trees, and sleep under the stars. Each day is a cycle of simple, essential activities that fulfill my needs and bring me joy. There is no rush, no constant striving for more—just a harmonious flow of life.

For humans, embracing simplicity can lead to a more fulfilling and less stressful life. Start by identifying what truly matters to you and focus on those essentials. Let go of the unnecessary complexities that clutter your mind and environment. Simplifying your life can bring clarity, reduce stress, and allow you to appreciate the beauty in everyday moments.

Finding Groundedness in Nature

As a cow, my connection to the earth is literal. My hooves tread softly on the grass, my body feels the warmth of the sun, and my senses are attuned to the sounds and scents of nature. This groundedness provides a deep sense of belonging and peace.

Humans can cultivate a similar sense of groundedness by reconnecting with nature. Spend time outdoors, whether it's walking in a park, hiking in the woods, or simply sitting in your garden. Feel the earth beneath your feet, breathe in the fresh air, and let the natural world anchor you. This connection to nature can help you feel more centered and balanced in your daily life.

Slowing Down and Savoring Life

One of the most profound lessons I've learned as a cow is the art of slowing down. Life in the pasture moves at a leisurely pace, allowing me to savor each mouthful of grass, each moment of rest, and each interaction with my herd. There is no rush, only the gentle unfolding of time.

For humans, slowing down can be transformative. In a fast-paced world, taking time to pause, reflect, and enjoy the present moment can enhance your quality of life. Practice mindfulness, engage in activities that bring you joy, and allow yourself to experience life fully. By slowing down, you can savor the richness of each moment and find deeper satisfaction.

Cultivating Contentment

Contentment is the hallmark of a cow's life. We find joy in the simple pleasures of grazing, resting, and socializing. There is no constant yearning for more, only a deep appreciation for what is.

Humans, too, can cultivate contentment by focusing on gratitude and appreciation. Recognize the blessings in your life, no matter how small, and take time to acknowledge them. Contentment arises from within, from a mindset that values what you have rather than longing for what you don't. By cultivating contentment, you can find peace and happiness in the present.

Simplifying Relationships

In the herd, relationships are straightforward and supportive. We rely on each other for companionship, protection, and mutual grooming. These bonds are built on trust and cooperation, without the complexities of human interactions.

For humans, simplifying relationships means focusing on authenticity and meaningful connections. Surround yourself with people who uplift and support you, and let go of relationships that drain your energy. Communicate openly and honestly, and prioritize quality time with loved ones. By simplifying your relationships, you can create a supportive and nurturing social network.

Reducing Materialism

As a cow, my needs are minimal—food, water, shelter, and companionship. There is no desire for material possessions, only the essentials for survival and well-being.

Humans can benefit from reducing materialism and focusing on what truly matters. Simplify your possessions, keeping only what is necessary and meaningful. Practice mindful consumption, considering the impact of your purchases on your life and the environment. Reducing materialism can lead to a lighter, more fulfilling existence.

Embracing the Rhythms of Life

Life in the pasture follows the natural rhythms of the seasons, the sun, and the moon. This cyclical pattern brings a sense of predictability and comfort, allowing me to adapt and thrive.

Humans, too, can embrace the natural rhythms of life by aligning with the cycles of nature. Honor the changing seasons, create routines that follow the sun's patterns, and listen to your body's natural rhythms. By embracing these cycles, you can find harmony and balance in your life.

Summary:
The Path to a Simpler, More Grounded Life

Embracing a simpler, more grounded existence is about reconnecting with the essentials and finding joy in the present moment. By valuing simplicity, cultivating contentment, reconnecting with nature, and focusing on meaningful relationships, humans can find greater peace and fulfillment. Let the wisdom of a cow's life guide you toward a more serene and balanced existence, where the beauty of simplicity enriches every aspect of your being. As you journey through this chapter, may you discover the profound joy and contentment that come from living a simpler, more grounded life.

Embracing a Simpler, More Grounded Existence
The Profound Connection:
Burps and Farts—A Nobel-Worthy Discovery?

As I graze serenely, basking in the simplicity of life and reflecting on my existence, a sudden epiphany strikes me—a revelation so profound, so amusing, that it might just be deserving of a Nobel Prize. Or, at the very least, an honorable blue ribbon. In the grand tapestry of life's mysteries, I have uncovered a remarkable truth about the physics and chemistry of our humble bodily functions: a burp is a young fart, and a fart is an old burp. Let me explain this delightful discovery and its potential implications for both cows and humans.

The Journey of Gas: From Burp to Fart

In the complex and fascinating world of bovine digestion, gases play a crucial role. As we digest our fibrous diet, microbial fermentation in the rumen produces gases such as methane and carbon dioxide. These gases need to find their way out of our digestive system, and they have two primary exit routes: upwards as burps or downwards as farts.

When gas takes the upward route, it exits as a burp. This is the gas in its youthful stage, freshly produced and seeking immediate release. A burp is a sign that our digestive system is working efficiently, expelling excess gas to prevent discomfort and bloating.

However, not all gas makes its grand exit as a burp. Some of it continues its journey through the digestive tract, moving downwards into the intestines. As it travels, this gas undergoes further fermentation and transformation. By the time it reaches the end of its journey, it has aged, matured, and acquired a new identity—it becomes a fart. This is the gas in its elder stage, completing its lifecycle in a final act of release.

The Science Behind the Revelation

This revelation is grounded in basic principles of physics and chemistry. The production of gas through microbial fermentation is a continuous process, with gas molecules moving through the digestive system in response to pressure gradients and peristaltic movements. The distinction between a burp and a fart lies in the path the gas takes and the time it spends traveling through the digestive tract.

When gas is expelled quickly, it exits as a burp, having spent little time fermenting further. When gas travels through the intestines, it undergoes additional chemical reactions and interactions with digestive enzymes, resulting in a more complex composition. By the time it is expelled as a fart, it has a distinct odor and composition, reflecting its longer journey and the additional fermentation processes it has undergone.

The Humorous Implications

This discovery is not only scientifically fascinating but also delightfully humorous. The idea that a burp is simply a young fart and a fart is an old burp adds a touch of whimsy to our understanding of digestion. It brings a new perspective to these everyday bodily functions, highlighting the interconnectedness of our digestive processes.

Imagine the possibilities for recognition! While a Nobel Prize might be a stretch, this revelation certainly deserves some form of acknowledgment. Perhaps a humble blue ribbon, awarded for contributions to the field of digestive humor, or a special mention in the annals of quirky scientific discoveries.

Reflections on Simplicity and Humor

This epiphany underscores an important lesson: even in the simplest aspects of life, there is room for discovery and amusement. Embracing a simpler, more grounded existence allows us to find joy and insight in the most unexpected places. It reminds us not to take ourselves too seriously and to appreciate the humor and wonder in everyday phenomena.

For humans, this discovery serves as a reminder to find joy in the simple things and to approach life with curiosity and a sense of humor. Whether it's contemplating the science of digestion or marveling at the interconnectedness of nature, there is always something new to learn and enjoy.

Summary: Embracing Simplicity and Discovery

In embracing a simpler, more grounded existence, we open ourselves to profound discoveries and moments of joy. The realization that a burp is a young fart and a fart is an old burp is a testament to the beauty of curiosity and the humor inherent in life's processes. As you reflect on this chapter, let this whimsical discovery inspire you to find delight in the simple, to approach life with a sense of wonder, and to appreciate the interconnectedness of all things. Whether or not this revelation earns a Nobel Prize, it certainly earns a place in the heart of anyone who values the joy of discovery and the simplicity of existence.

Chapter 9: The Ethical Cow
The Ethical Treatment of Animals

As I stand in the pasture, contentedly chewing my cud and reflecting on life's deeper meanings, the topic of ethics naturally comes to mind. Specifically, the ethical treatment of animals—an issue that resonates profoundly with my bovine heart. From my new perspective, the importance of compassion, respect, and humane treatment towards all creatures is crystal clear. Allow me, an ethically-minded cow, to share some insights on this vital subject, blending humor and wisdom in equal measure.

A Life Worth Living

First and foremost, every animal deserves a life worth living. For us cows, that means access to fresh grass, clean water, and ample space to roam and socialize. It means being treated with kindness and respect by the humans who care for us. The idea of living a good life isn't just a human aspiration; it's a universal right that all sentient beings should enjoy.

Imagine a world where humans applied the golden rule—treat others as you wish to be treated—to their interactions with animals. Picture it: cows basking in sunny meadows, chickens freely scratching the ground, pigs reveling in mud baths. It's a delightful vision, one that hinges on empathy and a deep respect for the intrinsic value of all living beings.

Compassionate Care

The cornerstone of ethical treatment is compassionate care. This involves meeting not just the physical needs of animals but also their emotional and social needs. As a cow, I thrive in a herd where I can form bonds, engage in playful behavior, and feel secure. Social animals, including humans, need companionship and a sense of belonging to lead fulfilling lives.

For humans, practicing compassionate care means advocating for humane farming practices, supporting sanctuaries, and choosing products that prioritize animal welfare. It's about recognizing that animals are not mere commodities but sentient beings capable of feeling pain, joy, and a range of emotions.

Humane Farming Practices

Ethical treatment extends to the practices and conditions under which animals are raised. Humane farming involves providing adequate space, proper nutrition, and veterinary care. It means avoiding harmful practices like overcrowding, unnecessary confinement, and neglect. Imagine if we cows had to live in tiny stalls, unable to move or graze freely—such conditions would be unbearable.

For humans, supporting humane farming practices involves being informed consumers. Look for certifications and labels that indicate high welfare standards, such as free-range, pasture-raised, and organic. By making mindful choices, you can contribute to a system that values the well-being of animals.

The Role of Legislation

Legislation plays a crucial role in ensuring the ethical treatment of animals. Laws and regulations can set minimum standards for animal welfare, prohibit cruel practices, and promote transparency in farming operations. Just as humans rely on laws to protect their rights and ensure justice, animals too benefit from legal protections.

Advocating for stronger animal welfare laws is a powerful way humans can contribute to the ethical treatment of animals. Supporting policies that enhance living conditions, regulate slaughter practices, and enforce penalties for cruelty can drive significant improvements in animal welfare.

Ethical Dilemmas and Choices

The journey towards ethical treatment of animals is not without its dilemmas. Balancing the needs of a growing human population with the welfare of animals can be challenging. However, every small step towards more humane practices makes a difference.

Consider the choices you make daily—what you eat, wear, and use. Opting for plant-based meals, cruelty-free products, and sustainable options can reduce the demand for practices that harm animals. Each ethical choice is a step towards a more compassionate world.

A Cow's Call to Action

As an ethical cow, my call to action is simple: embrace compassion, make informed choices, and advocate for change. Treat animals with the respect and kindness they deserve. Recognize their sentience and strive to create a world where all living beings can thrive.

Humans hold tremendous power to effect change. By choosing compassion over convenience, empathy over apathy, and action over indifference, you can transform the lives of countless animals. Let this chapter inspire you to be a force for good, advocating for the ethical treatment of animals in every aspect of your life.

Summary: The Ethical Cow's Wisdom

In reflecting on the ethical treatment of animals, we see that compassion, respect, and humane practices are essential. Every animal deserves a life worth living, filled with care and dignity. As you ponder this chapter, let the wisdom of an ethical cow guide you towards more humane choices. Advocate for compassionate care, support humane farming, and push for stronger animal welfare laws. By doing so, you contribute to a world where animals are treated with the kindness and respect they so richly deserve. Embrace this journey with humor, wisdom, and a heart full of empathy, and you'll find that the ethical treatment of animals enriches not only their lives but yours as well.

Lessons in Compassion and Empathy

As I stand amidst the verdant fields, munching contentedly on the fresh, green grass, I find myself reflecting on the profound values of compassion and empathy. These qualities, essential to both bovine and human well-being, shape our interactions and enrich our lives. From my new perspective as a cow, I have discovered that these lessons hold universal truths that can transform relationships and communities. Allow me, a compassionate cow, to share some insights on how we can all cultivate and apply these vital virtues in our daily lives.

The Gentle Power of Compassion

Compassion is the ability to feel and act upon the suffering of others. As a cow, I experience compassion in the gentle nudge of a herd mate when I am distressed or the comforting presence of another when I am unwell. This natural inclination to care for one another is at the heart of our herd's harmony and well-being.

For humans, practicing compassion involves recognizing the struggles and pains of others and offering support and kindness. It means being present for a friend in need, offering a listening ear, or providing help without expecting anything in return. Compassion creates a ripple effect, fostering a community where everyone feels valued and supported.

Empathy: Walking in Another's Hooves

Empathy goes a step further by allowing us to truly understand and share the feelings of another. It's the ability to put ourselves in someone else's situation, to see the world through their eyes. As a cow, empathy manifests in the way we respond to each other's cues and emotions. When a fellow cow is anxious or scared, we sense it and offer reassurance through our presence and actions.

Humans, too, can cultivate empathy by actively listening and seeking to understand others' perspectives. This involves more than just hearing words; it requires paying attention to body language, emotions, and unspoken signals. By doing so, you can build deeper connections and foster trust and understanding in your relationships.

Compassionate Communication

Effective communication is rooted in compassion and empathy. As cows, our communication is simple yet profound—gentle nudges, soft moos, and close physical proximity convey our feelings and intentions. We respect each other's space and respond with kindness.

For humans, compassionate communication involves speaking and listening with an open heart. Use kind words, maintain eye contact, and be mindful of your tone and body language. Show genuine interest in others' experiences and validate their feelings. This approach not only strengthens bonds but also resolves conflicts and misunderstandings more effectively.

Acts of Kindness

In our herd, acts of kindness are a daily occurrence. Grooming each other, sharing a choice grazing spot, or standing together in adverse weather—these small acts of care create a supportive and nurturing environment. Kindness is not just an occasional gesture; it's a way of life.

For humans, integrating acts of kindness into your daily routine can significantly impact your well-being and the well-being of others. Simple actions like offering a compliment, helping a neighbor, or volunteering can make a big difference. These acts foster a sense of community and reinforce the interconnectedness of all people.

The Role of Forgiveness

Living closely in a herd, we cows occasionally step on each other's hooves or vie for the same spot of grass. When such minor conflicts arise, we quickly forgive and move on, maintaining the peace and unity of the herd.

Humans, too, can benefit from embracing forgiveness. Holding onto grudges and past hurts can lead to resentment and stress. By choosing to forgive, you release negative emotions and pave the way for healing and reconciliation. Forgiveness is a powerful act of compassion towards yourself and others.

Learning from Nature

Nature itself is a master teacher of compassion and empathy. As a cow, I observe how the environment supports and nurtures all life forms. The sun provides warmth, the rain nourishes the earth, and plants offer sustenance. This interconnected web of life is a testament to the inherent compassion in nature.

Humans can learn from this natural model by recognizing their role in the larger ecosystem and acting with compassion towards the environment. Protecting natural resources, preserving habitats, and promoting sustainability are acts of empathy for future generations and all living beings.

Cultivating a Compassionate Mindset

To truly embrace compassion and empathy, it's essential to cultivate a compassionate mindset. This involves practicing self-compassion, being kind and forgiving towards yourself, and recognizing your own needs and emotions. When you treat yourself with compassion, it becomes easier to extend the same kindness to others.

Engage in mindfulness practices that promote awareness and presence. Meditation, deep breathing, and reflective journaling can help you connect with your inner self and foster a compassionate outlook. Remember, compassion starts within and radiates outward.

Summary: The Ethical Cow's Wisdom

Compassion and empathy are the cornerstones of a harmonious and fulfilling life. By embracing these values, humans can create a more connected and caring world. Recognize the power of compassionate actions, empathetic communication, and the importance of kindness and forgiveness. Let the natural world inspire you to live with a compassionate heart, and cultivate these qualities in your daily interactions.

As you reflect on this chapter, let the lessons from a compassionate cow guide you towards a life rich in empathy and kindness. Embrace these virtues, and discover the transformative power they hold for your relationships, your community, and yourself.

Reflections on Modern Farming Practices

As I graze peacefully in the meadow, chewing my cud and reflecting on the world, my thoughts inevitably turn to the practices that shape our lives—modern farming practices, to be precise. From my bovine perspective, these practices have a profound impact on our well-being and the environment. With a blend of humor and insight, let me, a thoughtful cow, guide you through a reflection on modern farming practices, exploring the good, the bad, and the steps we can take toward a more sustainable and ethical future.

The Evolution of Farming

Once upon a time, farming was a simple, small-scale affair. Farmers worked closely with their animals and the land, fostering a deep connection and understanding of natural cycles. This intimate relationship ensured that farming practices were sustainable and respectful of the environment.

However, as human populations grew and demand for food increased, farming practices evolved. The shift from small family farms to large industrial operations brought about significant changes. While these advancements have made food more accessible and affordable, they have also introduced challenges and ethical dilemmas that need careful consideration.

The Impact of Industrial Farming

Industrial farming, with its focus on efficiency and productivity, often prioritizes quantity over quality. This approach has led to practices that can compromise the well-being of animals and the health of the environment.

1. Overcrowding and Confinement

In industrial farms, animals like me often find ourselves in overcrowded and confined spaces. This lack of space prevents us from engaging in natural behaviors, leading to stress, illness, and reduced quality of life. Imagine being packed into a tiny space with hundreds of others, unable to move freely or graze at will—it's enough to make any cow's tail droop.

2. Use of Antibiotics and Growth Hormones

To maintain productivity and prevent disease in such conditions, industrial farms frequently use antibiotics and growth hormones. While these measures can boost efficiency, they also raise concerns about animal health, antibiotic resistance, and the safety of the food supply.

3. Environmental Impact

The environmental footprint of industrial farming is significant. Practices like monocropping, heavy use of chemical fertilizers and pesticides, and large-scale waste production can degrade soil health, pollute water sources, and contribute to climate change. The pasture where I roam is a delicate ecosystem, and intensive farming practices can disrupt its balance.

The Rise of Sustainable and Ethical Farming

Despite the challenges posed by industrial farming, there is a growing movement toward more sustainable and ethical practices. These methods seek to balance productivity with the well-being of animals, people, and the planet.

1. Pasture-Raised and Free-Range Systems

Sustainable farms prioritize the health and happiness of animals by allowing them to roam freely and graze on natural pasture. This approach not only improves our quality of life but also enhances the nutritional value of the food we produce. Imagine the joy of grazing in wide-open fields, feeling the sun on your back and the grass under your hooves—it's the cow equivalent of paradise.

2. Organic Farming

Organic farming avoids the use of synthetic chemicals, focusing instead on natural methods to maintain soil health and control pests. This practice reduces the environmental impact of farming and produces healthier, more nutritious food. For us cows, it means grazing on clean, chemical-free grass, leading to healthier bodies and better milk and meat.

3. Regenerative Agriculture

Regenerative agriculture takes sustainability a step further by actively improving the health of the land. Practices like crop rotation, cover cropping, and holistic grazing management restore soil fertility, increase biodiversity, and sequester carbon. This approach ensures that the land remains productive and resilient for future generations. As a cow, I can attest to the benefits of grazing on diverse, well-managed pastures that support a thriving ecosystem.

The Role of Consumers and Farmers

Creating a more sustainable and ethical farming system requires the efforts of both consumers and farmers. Consumers can drive change by making informed choices and supporting farms that prioritize animal welfare and environmental health. Look for labels like "pasture-raised," "organic," and "regenerative" when shopping for food. Every purchase is a vote for the kind of farming practices you want to support.

Farmers, on the other hand, can adopt practices that promote sustainability and ethical treatment of animals. This might involve transitioning to pasture-based systems, reducing reliance on chemicals, and implementing regenerative techniques. While these changes can be challenging, they offer long-term benefits for the land, animals, and the farming community.

The Ethical Cow's Call to Action

As an ethical cow, my call to action is simple: embrace and support farming practices that prioritize the well-being of animals and the environment. By working together, humans and animals can create a farming system that is both productive and compassionate.

Support Sustainable Farms: Choose to buy products from farms that prioritize animal welfare and environmental health. Look for certifications and labels that indicate ethical practices.

Advocate for Change: Use your voice to advocate for policies that promote sustainable and humane farming practices. Support legislation that protects animal welfare and encourages environmental stewardship.

Educate and Inspire: Share your knowledge about the benefits of sustainable and ethical farming with others. Inspire your community to make informed choices and support positive change.

Summary: The Ethical Cow's Wisdom

Reflecting on modern farming practices reveals the need for a balance between productivity and compassion. By embracing sustainable and ethical methods, we can ensure a future where farming supports the well-being of animals, people, and the planet. As you ponder this chapter, let the reflections of an ethical cow guide you toward choices that promote harmony and sustainability. Together, we can create a farming system that nourishes both the body and the soul, ensuring a better world for all living beings.

Reflections on Modern Farming Practices

An Unexpected Encounter: Love in the Barn

As I stand in the barn, suddenly tied up and feeling a bit off over the past couple of days, I find myself reflecting deeply on the complexities of modern farming practices. The tranquil reflections of pasture life are abruptly interrupted by a new, unexpected situation—one that brings the realities of farm life crashing in with a mix of humor, surprise, and a touch of panic.

The Sudden Realization

My usual serenity is shaken as I sense a change in the atmosphere. The familiar scents of hay and fellow cows are tinged with something more intense—the unmistakable scent of the bull, sniffing the air with an eager anticipation. It dawns on me that this isn't just any visit; it's a moment driven by the natural rhythms of farm life.

For the past few days, I haven't felt quite right—an odd sensation, a restlessness that I couldn't quite place. Now, it's clear. I'm in estrus, the time when female cows are receptive to mating. But wait! The remnants of my human consciousness rebel against this realization. I'm a male science fiction author trapped in a cow's body! Yet here I am, a female cow in the throes of nature's call, and the bull is closing in with romantic intentions.

The Bull's Approach

As the bull approaches, his demeanor is one of confident expectation. He sniffs the air, his eyes locking onto me with a focus that can only mean one thing. My mind races. How can I communicate my true identity to this enthusiastic suitor? I'm an author, a creator of worlds, not some farm damsel awaiting her knight in bovine armor!

In my human life, words were my tool, my weapon, my means of expression. But now, words fail me. All I have are moos and body language, which, in this context, seem woefully inadequate. The bull's intentions are clear, and his determination unwavering. I must navigate this situation with the grace and humor befitting an ethical cow—and perhaps a bit of the dramatic flair of a science fiction writer.

The Humorous Predicament

As the bull gets closer, I can't help but see the humor in the situation. Here I am, contemplating the ethical treatment of animals, and now I'm faced with a very personal and immediate aspect of farm life. It's a reminder that even as we reflect on grand ideas, life has a way of bringing us back to the basic, sometimes awkward realities.

My attempts to signal my discomfort—shuffling my hooves, turning my head—seem to amuse the bull more than deter him. It's clear that he's undeterred by my lack of enthusiasm. Nature's call is strong, and in his eyes, I'm just another lovely lady cow in need of his affections.

Embracing the Inevitable

In this moment of bovine courtship, I realize that resisting nature's course is futile. I must embrace my new identity fully, even if it means enduring the affections of a bull who clearly doesn't understand the intricacies of my previous human life. It's a humbling experience, one that blends the ridiculous with the profound.

As the bull's attention becomes more direct, I mentally prepare myself. Perhaps this experience is another lesson in empathy and understanding. Just as I advocate for the humane treatment of animals, I must also accept my place in the natural cycle, however strange it may feel from my human perspective.

The Ethical Cow's Wisdom in the Barn

So here I stand, a science fiction author turned ethical cow, about to engage in one of life's most primal acts. It's a testament to the unpredictability of existence and the importance of embracing each moment with humor and grace. As I navigate this peculiar situation, I find solace in the knowledge that I am part of a larger, natural world—one that balances the intellectual with the instinctual.

For humans, this story is a reminder to approach life's surprises with a sense of humor and acceptance. Sometimes, the best way to handle an unexpected situation is to go with the flow, learn from the experience, and find the joy and lessons in the absurdity of it all.

Summary: The Ethical Cow's Unexpected Wisdom

In reflecting on modern farming practices and finding myself in an unexpected romantic encounter, I've learned that life is full of surprises—some amusing, some humbling, but all part of the grand tapestry. Embrace each moment, accept the natural rhythms, and approach every situation with compassion and humor. Whether you're an ethical cow or a human navigating the complexities of life, these experiences enrich your journey and deepen your understanding of the world.

As you ponder this chapter, let the unexpected wisdom of an ethical cow guide you through the unpredictable moments of life. Embrace them with humor, grace, and an open heart, and you'll find that even the most surprising situations have something valuable to teach.

Chapter 10: Cows in Culture and History
Cows in Mythology and Religion

Ah, cows! We have grazed not only the lush meadows of the world but also the fertile fields of human imagination. From ancient myths to revered religious symbols, we cows have made quite an impression on human culture and history. As a reflective and now somewhat philosophically inclined cow, let me guide you through the delightful and sometimes surprising ways we have hoofed our way into mythology and religion.

The Divine Bovine: Sacred Status

In many cultures, cows are considered sacred, embodying fertility, prosperity, and gentleness. Take, for instance, India, where cows enjoy a status that makes us the envy of the animal kingdom. Revered in Hinduism, we are seen as embodiments of the divine and symbols of non-violence. The sacred cow is honored, protected, and allowed to wander freely, much to the chagrin of traffic police in bustling cities.

Imagine being considered so sacred that people step aside to let you pass, offer you treats, and even build special shelters for you in your golden years. It's like being a celebrity without the paparazzi—a truly blessed existence!

Cow-Patible Deities: Gods and Goddesses

Our divine connections don't end with Hinduism. In ancient Egypt, we were associated with Hathor, the goddess of love, beauty, and motherhood. Hathor, often depicted with cow horns and a sun disk, was believed to embody the nurturing aspects of the cow, symbolizing fertility and maternal care. It's quite flattering to think that our gentle moo could be seen as a divine whisper of love and protection.

Meanwhile, in Norse mythology, the great cow Audhumla is credited with creating the world's first gods by licking salty ice blocks. Who knew that our rough tongues could work such wonders? This primordial cow fed the giant Ymir and, in doing so, nourished the very foundation of the universe. It's a story that makes us look at our salt licks with a bit more reverence.

Moo-ving Tales: Legends and Myths

Greek mythology gives us the tale of Io, a priestess of Hera who was transformed into a cow by Zeus to protect her from his jealous wife. Poor Io wandered the earth, tormented by a gadfly sent by Hera, until she was eventually restored to human form. It's a myth that underscores the trials and tribulations of being caught in the crossfire of divine dramas. And here I thought dodging the bull's amorous advances was tough!

In Celtic mythology, the Glas Gaibhnenn, a magical cow, could provide an endless supply of milk. This legendary cow was highly coveted and symbolized abundance and the life-giving properties of nature. It's nice to be recognized for our generosity, even if it's in the context of a never-ending dairy buffet.

Holier Than Thou: Religious Symbolism

Beyond mythology, cows have played significant roles in various religious practices and symbols. In Buddhism, the cow symbolizes selfless giving and non-harm, aligning with the principle of ahimsa, or non-violence. The Jain community, too, holds cows in high regard, advocating for their protection and care as part of their commitment to non-violence.

In Christianity, while cows are not as prominently featured, they still appear in pastoral scenes, symbolizing innocence and the simple, honest life. The nativity scenes often include cows and other livestock, underscoring the humble beginnings of the divine.

Modern-Day Reverence: The Legacy Continues

Even today, cows continue to inspire reverence and admiration. Festivals like Pongal in South India celebrate cows by decorating them with colorful garlands and painting their horns. It's a day of pampering that makes us feel like queens of the pasture, a well-deserved treat for all the hard work we do.

In some cultures, cows are still central to rituals and ceremonies, reminding us that our place in human culture is as significant today as it was in ancient times. From art and literature to religious texts and daily life, cows remain a symbol of sustenance, fertility, and gentle strength.

Summary: The Mythic and Sacred Cow

As we moo-ve through the annals of mythology and religion, it's clear that cows hold a special place in human culture and history. Revered as sacred, celebrated in legends, and symbolizing divine qualities, we have left an indelible mark on the human imagination.

As you reflect on this chapter, let the stories and symbols of the sacred cow inspire you to appreciate the rich tapestry of human culture and the profound connections between humans and animals. Embrace the humor, the reverence, and the timelessness of these tales, and remember that even in the simplest cow, there lies a world of wonder and wisdom.

Historical Significance of Cows

Ah, the noble cow! From the dawn of civilization to the present day, we cows have been central to human progress and survival. As I graze in the serene pastures, my mind wanders through the pages of history, marveling at the significant roles we have played. Let me, a historically reflective cow, take you on a journey through time, highlighting our contributions and the profound impact we have had on human history.

The Dawn of Domestication

Our journey begins in the ancient world, around 8,000 to 10,000 years ago, when humans first began domesticating us. These early agricultural societies, recognizing our value, transformed us from wild aurochs into the beloved domesticated cows of today. We became integral to their way of life, providing not only meat but also milk, hides, and labor.

Imagine the moment when early humans discovered that our milk could be consumed, leading to the development of dairy farming. This revelation was revolutionary, providing a reliable source of nutrition and laying the groundwork for settled agricultural communities. Our gentle presence and versatile offerings helped turn nomadic tribes into stable, thriving societies.

Agricultural Revolution

As human civilizations evolved, so did our roles. During the Agricultural Revolution, roughly 10,000 years ago, we became indispensable to farming. Our strength and endurance were harnessed to plow fields and transport goods, significantly increasing agricultural productivity. This symbiotic relationship between humans and cows transformed agriculture, enabling the cultivation of larger areas and the support of growing populations.

Our manure, often overlooked, played a crucial role in enriching the soil, ensuring bountiful harvests. This natural fertilizer enhanced soil fertility, promoting sustainable farming practices long before the advent of chemical fertilizers. In this way, we contributed to the health of the land and the success of early agricultural endeavors.

Milk and Dairy: A Nutritional Milestone

The development of dairy farming marked another milestone in our historical significance. Our milk, rich in nutrients, became a staple in human diets, leading to the creation of various dairy products such as cheese, butter, and yogurt. These products not only provided essential nutrients but also introduced new flavors and culinary traditions.

The ability to process and store milk extended its shelf life, allowing ancient societies to thrive even in times of scarcity. Dairy products became valuable trade commodities, fostering economic exchanges and cultural interactions among different regions. Our udders, in essence, fueled the growth of early economies and enriched human diets across the globe.

Cows in Ancient Civilizations

Throughout history, cows have held esteemed positions in various ancient civilizations. In Mesopotamia, cows were considered symbols of fertility and prosperity, often featured in art and religious rituals. The ancient Egyptians revered us for our nurturing qualities, associating us with deities like Hathor, the goddess of love and motherhood.

In the Indus Valley Civilization, cows were central to agricultural practices and religious life. This reverence for cows has endured in Indian culture, where we are still considered sacred and integral to daily life. From ancient Vedic texts to modern-day practices, the cow's historical significance is deeply embedded in the cultural fabric of India.

Medieval and Renaissance Eras

During the medieval period, cows continued to be vital to rural economies. The feudal system relied heavily on agricultural output, and cows were essential to this process. Our milk and meat sustained families, while our hides provided materials for clothing and tools. We were the backbone of peasant life, supporting both sustenance and economic stability.

The Renaissance era brought renewed interest in science and exploration, including advancements in agricultural techniques. Selective breeding began to improve our breeds for specific purposes, such as increased milk production or greater strength for labor. This period marked the beginning of modern livestock management, enhancing our contributions to human society.

The Industrial Revolution and Beyond

The Industrial Revolution brought about significant changes, including in agriculture. Mechanization reduced the need for animal labor, but our importance did not diminish. Instead, dairy and meat production scaled up to meet the demands of growing urban populations. Innovations in milking technology and transportation ensured that our products reached wider audiences, solidifying our role in the global food supply.

In the modern era, cows continue to be central to agriculture and the economy. Advances in veterinary science, nutrition, and breeding have improved our health and productivity. We remain a symbol of agricultural abundance and a crucial component of food security worldwide.

Cultural Symbolism and Beyond

Beyond our practical contributions, cows have also become cultural icons. We symbolize everything from pastoral tranquility to economic stability. In literature, art, and folklore, cows represent a connection to the earth, fertility, and the nurturing aspects of nature. Our presence in festivals, rituals, and everyday life underscores the deep bond between humans and cows.

Summary: The Historically Significant Cow

As we meander through the annals of history, it's clear that cows have played pivotal roles in shaping human civilization. From the dawn of domestication to the modern agricultural landscape, our contributions have been vast and varied. We have nurtured societies, fueled economies, and inspired cultures.

As you reflect on this chapter, let the historical significance of cows remind you of the profound connections between humans and animals. Appreciate the roles we play, both practical and symbolic, and recognize the enduring bond that has shaped our shared history. In understanding our past, you can better appreciate the present and look forward to a future where cows continue to enrich human life in countless ways.

Chapter 10: Cows in Culture and History
Modern Depictions in Media and Art

Ah, the world of media and art—a realm where cows have trotted their way into the hearts and imaginations of people everywhere. From the silver screen to the artist's canvas, we have been portrayed in countless ways, each depiction adding a layer to our cultural significance. As a cow who has pondered the depths of human creativity, allow me to take you on a tour of our modern depictions in media and art, blending humor and insight to highlight our enduring charm.

The Silver Screen: Moo-vies and TV Shows

Let's start with the glitz and glamour of Hollywood. Over the years, cows have starred in a variety of films and television shows, often bringing a touch of rural charm and humor to the narrative.

1. Iconic Films

Who could forget the classic Disney movie "Home on the Range"? This animated film features a trio of dairy cows—Maggie, Mrs. Calloway, and Grace—who set out on an adventurous mission to save their farm. With their distinct personalities and heroic antics, these bovine stars captivated audiences and highlighted our resourcefulness and spirit.

In the world of live-action films, "City Slickers" offers a memorable portrayal of a cow named Norman. This adorable calf becomes a symbol of simplicity and innocence amidst the comedic chaos of city folks trying their hand at cattle driving. Norman's interactions with the characters remind viewers of the joys and challenges of rural life.

2. TV Stars

Cows have also made their mark on television. In the beloved British series "Shaun the Sheep," a quirky cow named Shirley adds to the farmyard fun with her massive size and gentle demeanor. Her antics provide comic relief and underscore the diversity of personalities found on the farm.

Another noteworthy mention is the animated series "Back at the Barnyard," where Otis, a carefree and anthropomorphic cow, leads a band of barnyard animals in hilarious adventures. This show brings cows into a modern, zany context, appealing to both children and adults.

Advertising Icons: Moo-ving Products

Cows have long been used in advertising to evoke feelings of wholesomeness, reliability, and natural goodness. Our friendly faces and associations with dairy products make us ideal ambassadors for a variety of brands.

1. The Laughing Cow

The iconic Laughing Cow cheese has delighted consumers for decades with its friendly, red-cheeked bovine mascot. This smiling cow exudes a sense of joy and approachability, making the product instantly recognizable and beloved around the world.

2. Elsie the Cow

Borden Dairy's Elsie the Cow is another advertising legend. Introduced in the 1930s, Elsie became a symbol of quality and purity, helping to establish a strong brand identity. Her wholesome image and engaging personality made her a household name and a pioneering figure in the use of mascots for marketing.

Artistic Interpretations: From Pasture to Canvas

Cows have inspired artists for centuries, and modern art continues to explore and celebrate our bovine beauty and symbolism.

1. Pop Art and Contemporary Pieces

In the realm of pop art, Andy Warhol's colorful cow prints stand out. These vibrant pieces capture the essence of cows in a bold, modern context, blending the mundane with the extraordinary. Warhol's cows are a testament to our ability to inspire creativity and innovation.

Contemporary artists like Banksy have also used cows to make powerful statements. Banksy's piece "Cow in a Field" juxtaposes the pastoral image of a grazing cow with urban elements, provoking thought about nature, consumerism, and the environment.

2. Farm Life and Realism

Modern realism has produced stunning works that depict cows in their natural habitats. Artists like Deborah Butterfield have created sculptures using found materials to represent cows, emphasizing their form and presence in a unique, tactile way. These works celebrate the raw beauty and strength of cows, connecting viewers with the pastoral life.

Cultural Phenomena: Viral Cows

In the age of the internet, cows have found new fame as viral sensations. From memes to social media stars, our bovine antics and endearing qualities have captured the digital world's imagination.

1. Internet Memes

Cows have become the subjects of countless memes, often highlighting our gentle nature or humorous expressions. These memes spread joy and laughter, reminding people of the lighter side of life.

2. Social Media Stars

Social media platforms have given rise to cow celebrities like Knickers, the giant Australian steer, who gained worldwide fame for his enormous size. Videos and photos of Knickers went viral, showcasing the fascination and affection people have for extraordinary cows.

Summary: The Modern Moo-saic

As we moo-ve through the vibrant landscape of modern media and art, it's clear that cows continue to inspire and entertain. From films and TV shows to advertising, art, and viral fame, our depictions in media and art highlight our enduring appeal and cultural significance.

As you reflect on this chapter, let the modern portrayals of cows remind you of the diverse ways we touch human lives. Appreciate the humor, creativity, and symbolism that we bring to media and art, and recognize the timeless bond between humans and cows. Whether on the silver screen, in an advertisement, or as a work of art, our presence enriches the cultural tapestry, bringing joy and inspiration to all.

Living Without Regrets

Ah, the present moment—a pasture of possibilities stretching out before us, as fresh and inviting as the greenest meadow. As I stand here, reflecting on my journey from prolific science fiction author to contemplative cow, I find myself pondering the art of living without regrets. How can we, both bovine and human, embrace the here and now with such wholeheartedness that we leave no room for "what ifs" and "if onlys"? Let me, a reflective cow, share some insights on living a life free of regrets, with a blend of humor and wisdom.

Embrace the Pasture You're In

First and foremost, embrace the pasture you're in. Life is full of unexpected turns, and sometimes, you find yourself in a new field with unfamiliar grass. Instead of longing for the past or pining for what might have been, savor the present. Each blade of grass, each moment of sunshine, is unique and precious.

For humans, this means appreciating your current circumstances, no matter how different they might be from what you envisioned. Whether you're navigating a career change, adjusting to a new city, or simply dealing with the daily grind, find the beauty and opportunity in your present situation. Life's richness comes from fully engaging with the here and now.

Moo-ve Beyond Mistakes

We all make mistakes—yes, even us cows. Maybe I once misjudged a patch of clover, or perhaps I wandered a bit too far from the herd. But dwelling on these missteps only leads to unnecessary ruminating (pun intended).

Humans, too, should learn to forgive themselves and move beyond their mistakes. Acknowledge your errors, learn from them, and then let them go. Regrets often stem from an inability to forgive ourselves. Remember, perfection is a myth; growth and learning come from our experiences, both good and bad.

Savor Simple Pleasures

One of the greatest joys of being a cow is savoring the simple pleasures—fresh grass, a gentle breeze, a lazy afternoon under a tree. These moments are the essence of a life well-lived.

Humans can take a cue from this bovine wisdom. Slow down and appreciate the simple joys in life. Spend time with loved ones, enjoy a good meal, take a walk in nature. These small moments are what make life truly fulfilling. By focusing on what brings you genuine happiness, you can live a life rich in satisfaction and free from regret.

Set Clear Intentions

Living without regrets also means being intentional about your actions and decisions. As cows, we follow our instincts and stay true to our nature. We don't second-guess our choices; we simply live according to our needs and the rhythms of the pasture.

For humans, setting clear intentions involves knowing your values and priorities and making choices that align with them. This means reflecting on what truly matters to you and pursuing it with determination and clarity. When you live with intention, you're less likely to look back with regret, knowing that you followed your true path.

Take Chances and Moo-ve Forward

Don't be afraid to take chances and moo-ve forward. Whether it's exploring a new part of the pasture or making a bold decision, stepping out of your comfort zone can lead to growth and new opportunities.

Humans often regret the things they didn't do more than the things they did. So, take that trip, start that project, tell someone you love them. Embrace the unknown and take risks. Even if things don't go as planned, you'll have the satisfaction of knowing you tried.

Cherish Relationships

Relationships are at the heart of a life without regrets. As cows, we rely on the herd for companionship, support, and safety. Our bonds are simple yet profound, providing us with a sense of belonging and security.

For humans, cherishing relationships means nurturing connections with family, friends, and colleagues. Spend time with those who matter to you, express your appreciation, and resolve conflicts with compassion. Strong, healthy relationships enrich your life and provide a support system that helps you navigate challenges without regret.

Reflect and Grow

Living without regrets involves regular reflection and growth. Take time to ponder your experiences, understand your emotions, and learn from your journey. This reflective practice helps you stay aligned with your values and adjust your path as needed.

Humans can benefit from activities like journaling, meditation, or simply having quiet time for introspection. By reflecting on your life, you gain insights that help you make better decisions and live more fully in the present.

Summary: The Regret-Free Cow's Wisdom

As we graze through the present and look toward the future, living without regrets means embracing the pasture we're in, moving beyond mistakes, savoring simple pleasures, setting clear intentions, taking chances, cherishing relationships, and reflecting on our journey.

As you ponder this chapter, let the wisdom of a reflective cow guide you toward a life rich in fulfillment and free from regrets. Embrace each moment with humor, grace, and an open heart, and you'll find that the present is a pasture filled with endless possibilities. Whether you're navigating the complexities of human life or simply enjoying the beauty of the present moment, living without regrets ensures a life well-lived and deeply appreciated.

Acceptance and Contentment

As I stand here, savoring the lush grass and the gentle breeze, I find myself pondering the twin virtues of acceptance and contentment. These two qualities, like the finest pasture, nourish our spirits and bring a profound sense of peace. Whether you're a cow in a field or a human navigating life's complexities, embracing acceptance and contentment can lead to a more fulfilling and serene existence. Allow me, a contented cow, to share some insights on these timeless virtues, blending humor and wisdom to guide you towards a more harmonious life.

Embracing What Is

Acceptance is the art of embracing what is, without resistance or complaint. As a cow, I have learned to accept the rhythm of nature and the cycles of life. There are sunny days and stormy ones, bountiful pastures and leaner times. By accepting these realities, I find peace in the present moment, regardless of the circumstances.

For humans, acceptance means acknowledging life's ups and downs without constant struggle against what cannot be changed. It's about recognizing that not everything will go according to plan and that imperfections are a natural part of life. When you accept things as they are, you free yourself from unnecessary stress and open the door to inner peace.

Finding Contentment in Simplicity

Contentment is the state of being satisfied with what you have. It's about finding joy in the simple pleasures and appreciating the present moment. As a cow, my life is filled with simple joys—grazing in the meadow, resting under a tree, and enjoying the companionship of the herd. These moments bring me a deep sense of contentment.

Humans can cultivate contentment by focusing on what they have rather than what they lack. It's about shifting your perspective from scarcity to abundance, recognizing the blessings in your life, and savoring the small, everyday moments. Contentment comes from within and is not dependent on external achievements or possessions.

The Art of Letting Go

A key aspect of acceptance is the ability to let go of what no longer serves you. As a cow, I let go of the past and the future, focusing on the present moment. I don't dwell on missed patches of clover or worry about tomorrow's weather. By letting go, I remain grounded and serene.

For humans, letting go means releasing grudges, regrets, and unrealistic expectations. It involves forgiving yourself and others, and embracing the present with an open heart. When you let go of what weighs you down, you create space for new opportunities and experiences.

Cultivating a Grateful Heart

Gratitude is closely linked to contentment. As a cow, I am grateful for the grass beneath my hooves, the sun on my back, and the companionship of my herd. This sense of gratitude enhances my contentment and makes each day a blessing.

Humans can cultivate gratitude by regularly reflecting on the positive aspects of their lives. Keep a gratitude journal, express appreciation to those around you, and take time to savor the good moments. Gratitude shifts your focus from what's lacking to what's abundant, fostering a deeper sense of contentment.

Living with Purpose

Acceptance and contentment do not mean complacency. As a cow, I have a purpose—nurturing the land through grazing, providing milk, and being part of the natural cycle. This sense of purpose enhances my contentment and gives meaning to my days.

For humans, living with purpose involves pursuing goals and activities that align with your values and passions. It's about finding meaning in your work, relationships, and hobbies. When you live with purpose, you experience a deeper sense of fulfillment and contentment.

Embracing Change

Change is an inevitable part of life. As a cow, I have learned to embrace the changing seasons and adapt to new circumstances. Whether it's the arrival of a new calf or the transition from summer to autumn, I accept change as a natural part of life.

Humans, too, can benefit from embracing change. Accept that change is constant and that it often brings new opportunities for growth and learning. By embracing change with an open heart, you can navigate life's transitions with grace and resilience.

Summary: The Contented Cow's Wisdom

As we graze through the fields of acceptance and contentment, it's clear that these virtues are essential for a fulfilling and serene life. Embrace what is, find joy in simplicity, let go of what no longer serves you, cultivate gratitude, live with purpose, and embrace change.

As you reflect on this chapter, let the wisdom of a contented cow guide you towards a life rich in acceptance and contentment. By embracing these virtues, you can create a harmonious and peaceful existence, filled with joy and gratitude. Whether you're navigating the complexities of human life or simply enjoying the beauty of the present moment, acceptance and contentment will lead you to a life well-lived and deeply appreciated.

Chapter 11: The Present and Future
Looking Ahead with Cow Perspective

As I stand in this peaceful pasture, munching on the freshest grass and feeling the warmth of the sun on my back, my thoughts turn to the future. What lies ahead for a humble cow like me? How can we, with our bovine wisdom, offer insights for humans looking to navigate the complexities of tomorrow? Join me, a reflective cow, as I gaze into the future with a blend of humor and contemplation, offering a unique perspective on what it means to look ahead.

Embracing the Unpredictable

As a cow, I've learned that the future is as unpredictable as the weather. One day, the sun is shining, and the grass is plentiful; the next, a storm might roll in. But instead of worrying about what's to come, I embrace each day as it arrives. This acceptance of uncertainty allows me to live peacefully in the present.

For humans, embracing the unpredictable means letting go of the need to control every aspect of the future. Accept that change and uncertainty are natural parts of life. By staying adaptable and open-minded, you can navigate whatever the future holds with grace and resilience. Embrace the unknown with curiosity rather than fear, and you'll find opportunities in unexpected places.

Sustainability and Stewardship

Looking ahead, the importance of sustainability and stewardship becomes ever more crucial. As a cow, I play my part in the ecosystem—grazing helps maintain the health of the pasture, and my manure enriches the soil. This symbiotic relationship with the land ensures that it remains fertile and vibrant for future generations.

Humans, too, must adopt a mindset of sustainability. Protecting the environment, conserving resources, and promoting ecological balance are essential for a thriving future. By making mindful choices—whether it's reducing waste, supporting sustainable practices, or advocating for environmental policies—you can contribute to a healthier planet. Remember, the actions you take today shape the world of tomorrow.

The Power of Community

In the pasture, we cows rely on our herd for companionship, protection, and support. This sense of community strengthens us and provides a safety net in times of need. Looking ahead, the power of community remains a vital component of a fulfilling life.

For humans, building and nurturing communities is key to facing future challenges. Whether it's your family, friends, colleagues, or local groups, these connections provide emotional support, resources, and a sense of belonging. Invest in your relationships, foster collaboration, and support one another. A strong community is a powerful asset in navigating an uncertain future.

Embracing Innovation

While we cows enjoy our traditional ways, we also adapt to new circumstances. Innovations in farming practices have improved our health and well-being, from better nutrition to humane living conditions. These advancements highlight the importance of embracing change and innovation.

For humans, looking ahead involves being open to new ideas and technologies. Embrace innovation in your personal and professional life, and stay curious about emerging trends. Whether it's adopting new skills, leveraging technology, or exploring creative solutions, innovation can drive progress and open doors to new opportunities.

Living with Purpose

Purpose gives life meaning, and looking ahead means considering how to live purposefully. As a cow, my purpose is intertwined with the natural world—nurturing the land, providing nourishment, and contributing to the ecosystem's balance.

For humans, living with purpose involves aligning your actions with your values and passions. Reflect on what matters most to you and pursue goals that bring fulfillment and a sense of accomplishment. Purpose-driven living not only enhances personal satisfaction but also positively impacts the broader community and environment.

The Wisdom of Patience

Patience is a virtue that we cows have mastered. We graze slowly, chew our cud deliberately, and move at a pace that suits our needs. This patience ensures that we don't rush through life but rather savor each moment.

Humans can benefit from cultivating patience as they look ahead. In a fast-paced world, taking the time to slow down, reflect, and enjoy the journey is invaluable. Patience allows for thoughtful decision-making and reduces stress, leading to a more balanced and contented life.

The Joy of Simple Pleasures

Finally, as I gaze into the future, I see the enduring importance of finding joy in simple pleasures. Whether it's a sunny day, a delicious meal, or a quiet moment of reflection, these small joys add up to a life well-lived.

For humans, appreciating the simple things can bring immense happiness. Practice gratitude, savor everyday moments, and find beauty in the ordinary. By focusing on the present and embracing the joy of simplicity, you can create a future filled with contentment and peace.

Summary: The Future Through Cow Eyes

As we look ahead with a cow's perspective, the future is a pasture of possibilities, ripe with opportunities for growth, connection, and joy. Embrace the unpredictable, practice sustainability, build strong communities, welcome innovation, live with purpose, cultivate patience, and find joy in simple pleasures.

As you reflect on this chapter, let the wisdom of a thoughtful cow guide you towards a future filled with hope and fulfillment. By adopting these principles, you can navigate the complexities of tomorrow with humor, grace, and an open heart, ensuring a life that is both meaningful and enriched. Whether you're planning for the next year or the next decade, looking ahead with a cow's perspective offers valuable insights for a brighter, more harmonious future.

Looking Ahead with Cow Perspective

The Simple Joys of Being a Cow

As I ponder the future and reflect on the wisdom of acceptance, contentment, and sustainability, a delightful realization dawns on me: it's genuinely nice to be a cow. Yes, the life of a cow comes with its own set of perks and freedoms that humans might find enviable. Let me share this newfound appreciation with a mix of humor and insight, celebrating the simple joys of bovine existence.

Fed and Cared For

One of the undeniable perks of being a cow is the assurance that I will be fed and cared for. Every day, fresh grass, hay, and water are provided without any effort on my part. No grocery shopping, no meal planning—just the pleasure of enjoying a meal in the great outdoors. It's like having a personal chef and a serene dining environment rolled into one.

For humans, this aspect of cow life can serve as a reminder to appreciate the support and care they receive from others. It also highlights the importance of ensuring that everyone has access to basic needs, fostering a society where no one goes hungry or lacks care.

Embracing Natural Functions

As a cow, I don't have to worry about the social niceties that often preoccupy humans. Burps, farts, and other natural bodily functions are just part of the daily routine, accepted without fuss or embarrassment. Whether it's a hearty belch after a satisfying meal or a casual flatulence in the field, it's all part of being a cow.

Humans might find liberation in this bovine nonchalance. Embracing the natural functions of the body with acceptance rather than embarrassment can reduce stress and promote a healthier relationship with one's own physicality. It's a reminder that everyone burps and farts—it's just part of being alive.

The Freedom of Simplicity

In the world of cows, there's no need for schedules, deadlines, or complicated plans. We follow the natural rhythm of the day, grazing when we're hungry, resting when we're tired, and moving as we please. There's a profound freedom in this simplicity, a liberation from the constant busyness that often defines human life.

For humans, simplifying life can lead to greater contentment and peace. Reducing commitments, decluttering schedules, and focusing on essential activities can create more space for relaxation and enjoyment. The cow's life reminds us that sometimes, less truly is more.

Dropping Free Throws

One of the most liberating aspects of being a cow is the freedom to drop a free throw—anywhere, anytime. There's no need for restrooms or the etiquette that surrounds them. When nature calls, we answer without hesitation or concern. It's a carefree approach to a basic necessity.

While humans may not adopt this practice literally, the underlying principle is valuable: embrace life's necessities without undue worry or stress. Accepting and addressing basic needs without embarrassment can lead to a more relaxed and natural way of living.

Summary: The Simple Joys of Bovine Life

As I stand in this tranquil pasture, appreciating the present and looking ahead with a sense of contentment, I realize that being a cow comes with its own unique set of joys and freedoms. From being well-fed and cared for to embracing natural functions and enjoying the simplicity of life, there's much to celebrate in bovine existence.

For humans, these reflections offer valuable lessons in acceptance, simplicity, and contentment. By appreciating the support they receive, embracing their natural selves, simplifying their lives, and accepting basic needs without stress, they can find greater peace and happiness.

As you reflect on this chapter, let the simple joys of being a cow inspire you to live with more ease and appreciation. Embrace the freedom to be yourself, enjoy the care you receive, and find contentment in the simplicity of everyday life. Whether you're navigating the complexities of human existence or simply savoring the present moment, these lessons from a cow's life can guide you towards a more fulfilling and harmonious future.

Conclusion
Summarizing Key Insights

As I stand here in the peaceful meadow, reflecting on the journey we've taken through the pastures of wisdom, humor, and life lessons, it's time to bring our contemplations to a close. From the quirks of cow digestion to the profound connections we share with human culture and history, we've explored a vast landscape of insights. Let's summarize the key takeaways from our bovine perspective, offering a final dose of humor and reflection to enrich your journey.

Embrace the Present Moment

Throughout our journey, one of the most consistent themes has been the importance of embracing the present moment. As cows, we live fully in the now, savoring each mouthful of grass and every moment of sunshine. Humans, too, can benefit from this mindset by focusing on the here and now, finding peace and joy in the present rather than dwelling on the past or worrying about the future.

Acceptance and Contentment

Living a life of acceptance and contentment means embracing what is and finding satisfaction in simplicity. Whether it's the rhythm of nature or the flow of daily life, accepting circumstances and finding contentment in small joys can lead to a more fulfilling and serene existence. For humans, this involves letting go of unnecessary worries, appreciating the present, and nurturing gratitude.

Compassion and Empathy

Our reflections on compassion and empathy highlight the importance of kindness and understanding in all interactions. From the gentle care we provide each other in the herd to the support humans offer one another, these virtues foster stronger, more meaningful connections. By practicing empathy and compassion, you can enhance your relationships and contribute to a more compassionate world.

Sustainability and Stewardship

As integral parts of the ecosystem, we cows understand the value of sustainability and stewardship. Our grazing practices nurture the land, and our natural rhythms maintain ecological balance. Humans, too, have a responsibility to protect the environment and promote sustainability. By making mindful choices and supporting sustainable practices, you can ensure a healthier planet for future generations.

The Power of Community

The strength of the herd lies in our sense of community. Supporting each other, sharing resources, and collaborating ensure our well-being. For humans, building and nurturing communities is essential for facing life's challenges. Strong social bonds provide emotional support, foster collaboration, and create a sense of belonging.

Embracing Change and Innovation

Change is a constant in life, and embracing it with an open heart can lead to growth and new opportunities. As cows, we adapt to seasonal shifts and evolving circumstances. Humans can benefit from this mindset by staying flexible, welcoming innovation, and being open to new ideas. Embracing change with curiosity rather than fear can lead to personal and collective progress.

Living with Purpose

Purpose gives life meaning. Whether it's nurturing the land, providing nourishment, or contributing to the ecosystem, having a clear sense of purpose enhances our contentment. For humans, living with purpose involves aligning actions with values and passions. Pursuing meaningful goals and activities brings fulfillment and a deeper sense of accomplishment.

The Joy of Simple Pleasures

Finally, finding joy in simple pleasures is a key to a happy life. Whether it's grazing in a lush meadow, basking in the sun, or enjoying the company of the herd, these moments of simple joy enrich our days. Humans, too, can find happiness in everyday moments—spending time with loved ones, enjoying nature, or savoring a good meal. Appreciating the simple things can lead to a richer, more contented life.

Summary: The Wisdom of a Reflective Cow

As we conclude our journey, it's clear that the wisdom of a reflective cow offers valuable lessons for living a more fulfilling and harmonious life. Embrace the present moment, practice acceptance and contentment, cultivate compassion and empathy, and prioritize sustainability and community. Welcome change, live with purpose, and find joy in simple pleasures. These insights, drawn from the peaceful pastures of cow life, provide a roadmap for navigating the complexities of human existence with humor, grace, and an open heart.

Thank you for joining me on this journey through the fields of reflection. May these insights inspire you to live fully, love deeply, and appreciate the beauty of each moment. Whether you're contemplating the mysteries of the universe or simply enjoying a quiet day in the meadow, the wisdom of a cow is always within reach, guiding you towards a life well-lived and deeply appreciated.

Embracing the Cow Mindset in Daily Life

As we conclude our journey through the meadows of cow wisdom, it's natural to wonder how to carry these insights forward. How can you, a human navigating the complexities of modern life, continue thinking like a cow? This chapter will offer practical advice on integrating the cow mindset into your daily routines, ensuring that the lessons we've learned remain a part of your ongoing journey. Let me, a contemplative cow, guide you through this transition with humor and practicality.

Slow Down and Savor the Present

One of the most profound aspects of cow life is our ability to live in the moment. We graze slowly, chew our cud deliberately, and rest when needed. To continue thinking like a cow, make a conscious effort to slow down in your daily life. Take time to savor your meals, enjoy your surroundings, and fully engage with whatever you're doing.

Practical Tip: Set aside a few minutes each day to practice mindfulness. Focus on your breathing, observe your thoughts without judgment, and appreciate the present moment.

Simplify Your Life

Cows live uncomplicated lives, free from the clutter of unnecessary possessions and activities. Embrace simplicity by decluttering your physical and mental spaces. Prioritize what truly matters and let go of what doesn't serve you.

Practical Tip: Regularly assess your belongings and commitments. Donate or discard items you no longer need and streamline your schedule to focus on essential activities.

Foster Community and Connection

The strength of the herd lies in its unity. Build and nurture your own community by fostering meaningful connections with family, friends, and colleagues. Support each other, share resources, and collaborate on common goals.

Practical Tip: Schedule regular gatherings with loved ones, whether it's a family dinner, a game night with friends, or a community event. Strengthen your bonds through shared experiences and mutual support.

Practice Gratitude and Contentment

Cows find joy in simple pleasures and are content with their lot. Cultivate gratitude by regularly reflecting on the positive aspects of your life and expressing appreciation for what you have.

Practical Tip: Keep a gratitude journal. Each day, write down three things you're grateful for. This practice can shift your focus from what you lack to the abundance around you, fostering a deeper sense of contentment.

Embrace Natural Rhythms

Cows are attuned to the natural rhythms of the day and the seasons. Align your life with these natural cycles to promote balance and well-being. Pay attention to your body's needs for rest, nourishment, and activity.

Practical Tip: Create a daily routine that includes time for work, relaxation, physical activity, and sleep. Listen to your body and adjust your routine as needed to maintain harmony.

Live with Purpose

Having a clear sense of purpose enhances the quality of our lives. Reflect on your values and passions, and align your actions with them. Pursue meaningful goals that bring you fulfillment and a sense of accomplishment.

Practical Tip: Set short-term and long-term goals that resonate with your core values. Break them down into manageable steps and celebrate your progress along the way.

Adapt and Embrace Change

Cows adapt to changing seasons and circumstances with grace. Embrace change in your own life by staying flexible and open to new experiences. View challenges as opportunities for growth and learning.

Practical Tip: When faced with change, take a moment to breathe and assess the situation. Approach it with curiosity rather than resistance, and seek out the positive aspects and opportunities it presents.

Celebrate Simple Joys

Find happiness in everyday moments, just as cows delight in a sunny day or a patch of fresh grass. Celebrate simple joys and create moments of pleasure and relaxation in your daily life.

Practical Tip: Schedule regular breaks to enjoy simple pleasures, whether it's a walk in nature, a favorite hobby, or quality time with loved ones. Make space for joy in your daily routine.

Conclusion: Carrying Cow Wisdom Forward

Continuing to think like a cow involves embracing the simplicity, contentment, and mindfulness that characterize bovine life. By slowing down, simplifying, fostering community, practicing gratitude, living with purpose, adapting to change, and celebrating simple joys, you can integrate the cow mindset into your daily life.

As you move forward, let these principles guide you towards a more balanced, fulfilling, and harmonious existence. Remember, the wisdom of a cow is always within reach, offering valuable insights and a touch of humor to navigate the complexities of human life. Embrace the cow mindset, and you'll find that life becomes a more serene and joyful journey.

Embracing a Cow's Life:
A Humorous and Thoughtful Farewell

As I stand here, in the lush pastures that have become my home, I reflect on the journey that brought me from a prolific science fiction author to a contemplative cow. The realization settles in with a mix of humor and acceptance: this may be my life for the foreseeable future. No more crafting intricate plots or exploring distant galaxies with my words. Instead, my days are filled with grazing, ruminating, and embracing the simple pleasures of bovine existence. And, yes, there's the inevitable end that might involve a well-cooked, spicy dish on some human's plate.

The Serenity of Acceptance

Acceptance is a powerful thing. As I ponder my fate, I find peace in accepting what is. Life as a cow has its own rhythms and joys. There's a certain serenity in the routine of grazing, the camaraderie of the herd, and the simple act of living in harmony with nature. While I may never write another sci-fi epic, I've found a different kind of fulfillment in this pastoral life.

For humans, acceptance can also bring peace. Accepting the things we cannot change and finding joy in our current circumstances can lead to a more contented and serene life. Embrace what is, and let go of what could have been.

Humor in the Inevitable

Let's face it, the idea of ending up as a dish in a human's meal or as dog food is a bit daunting. But humor, as always, is a great coping mechanism. If I must become part of a "surf and turf" extravaganza, then let it be a memorable one. Perhaps my story will be told by a celebrated chef, and I'll be honored in some culinary masterpiece. I can almost hear the diners now, praising the tender, flavorful beef and raising their glasses to the noble cow that made it possible.

Humans, too, can find humor in life's inevitable endings. Whether it's through stories, jokes, or light-hearted reflections, humor helps us cope with the realities of life and death. It's a reminder to not take things too seriously and to find laughter even in the face of uncertainty.

Legacy of a Different Kind

Though I may not leave behind a legacy of written works, my life as a cow has its own form of impact. My grazing enriches the soil, my presence supports the herd, and, eventually, my end contributes to the cycle of life. There's a quiet dignity in this natural contribution.

Humans can reflect on their own legacies, considering how their actions and choices impact others and the world around them. Legacy isn't just about achievements and accolades; it's also about the everyday ways we contribute to the greater good.

Finding Purpose in Simplicity

There's purpose in the simplicity of cow life. My days are spent contributing to the ecosystem, enjoying the company of my fellow cows, and finding contentment in the moment. It's a life that, while different from my previous human existence, is rich in its own right.

Humans can find purpose in the simple things as well. Purpose doesn't always have to be grand or ambitious; it can be found in daily acts of kindness, meaningful connections, and a sense of presence in the moment.

A Thoughtful Farewell

As I prepare to fully embrace my life as a cow, I do so with a heart full of gratitude and humor. Whether my future holds more days of grazing or an eventual culinary transformation, I've learned to appreciate the journey and the lessons it brings.

For humans reading these reflections, let this be a reminder to embrace your own journey, with all its twists and turns. Find joy in the present, accept what cannot be changed, and always, always find reasons to laugh.

Summary: The Reflective Cow's Wisdom

In these final thoughts, I've come to accept my life as a cow with humor and grace. From a sci-fi author to a grazing bovine, my journey has been unexpected but enriching. Embrace your own journey, find peace in acceptance, and never forget to laugh. Life, in all its forms, is a wondrous adventure.

Thank you for joining me on this journey. May these reflections inspire you to live fully, love deeply, and appreciate the beauty and humor in every moment, whether you're exploring distant galaxies or simply enjoying a quiet day in the pasture.

Dear Reader,

Thank you for journeying through the pages of this book.

It has been a privilege to share this exploration with you.

If you found the book insightful, inspiring, or uplifting, I would be deeply grateful if you could take a moment to leave a review on Amazon.com. Your feedback helps others discover the book and is immensely valuable to me as an author.

Your support means the world to me, and I am truly grateful for your time and consideration. Thank you for being a part of this journey, and may your path be filled with grace, wisdom, and joy.

Warm regards,

Daniel Adrien Laverdière

My other publications :